Creative Jamaican

COOKING & MENUS

Real Jamaican Cooking with Authentic Jerk Recipes

NEW EDITION

Over 100,000 copies in print.

by the late Master Chef Leonard 'Sonny' Henry,
Mike and Dawn Henry

LMH Publishing Limited

Editor: Charles-Anthony Moore
Cover Designer; LeeQuee Design
Text Design and Layout: Sanya Dockery

Coverphotos Courtesy of the Jamaica Observer.
Inside Photos Courtesy of Sandals Royal Caribbean (Bahamas)

Published by:
LMH Publishing Ltd.
Building # 10
7-9 Norman Road,
Kingston, CSO
Email: lmhbookpublishing@cwjamaica.com

Printed & Bound in China   ISBN 976-8202-07-6

This new and revised edition commemorates the life of Master Chef 'Sonny' Henry, whose artistry in the kitchen was recognized by those who visited Saffrons in St. Petersburg, Florida and before that, the "Old Homestead" Steak House and Mike's Nyamburghers in Jamaica.

With his passing, Sonny's role has been adopted by his sister-in-law Dawn Henry who adds the modern spice of good down home Jamaican Cooking.

CONTENTS

FOREWORD

This is a cookbook devoted to people who delight in tasty, spicy food. The special sections on Jerk cooking, Barbecues and Menus, will be a helpful aid to those who enjoy entertaining. The index also makes the book a useful reference for those interested in serious cuisine.

The recipes in the book reflect to a large extent the cultural heritage of the people in Jamaica: thus you will find recipes that reflect the Indian, African, European and both North and Latin American aspects of its culinary character following the Jamaican motto "Out Of Many One People". Many of the dishes have been adapted to make use of the foods we grow, such as ackee, plantain, coconut, paw-paw, mango, cassava and many others, which are considered exotic in other parts of the world.

For our foreign visitors who wish to prepare at home some of the dishes they may have tasted in restaurants or hotels, this book will be a handy guide. In many cases, they will be able to find the ingredients they need in their local markets or West Indian communities.

For those who live here, may this book encourage a new and happy familiarity with foods we grow.

The Publishers

This book is one in a series of cookbooks which are:
Caribbean Cooking and Menus
Bahamian Cooking and Menus
Creative Jamaican Cooking and Menus

Appetizers & Hors D'oeuvres

ROASTED BREADFRUIT

1 3 lb. ripe breadfruit   1   tbsp. vegetable oil

1. Preheat oven to 350°F.
2. Oil breadfruit and, with a knife, make a cross at the top and bottom of the fruit. The cross at the top and bottom of the breadfruit allows steam to escape while baking.
3. Bake on a greased baking sheet for 1½ to 2 hours, until fruit yields to the pressure of your thumb.
4. Cool slightly, peel, and wrap in a damp dishcloth until you are ready to serve.
5. To serve, slice thinly, cutting away centre core.

Leftover breadfruit can be deep-fried, sprinkled with salt, and served with breakfast.

CURRIED CODFISH

½ lb. salt codfish   1   teaspoon lime juice
2 tablespoons minced onion   *   flour
1 tablespoon curry powder   *   oil

1. Wash fish, and cut into strips. Flour lightly and fry in bubbling oil.
2. Take out the fish. Fry onion in the pan.
3. Sprinkle with curry powder and moisten with lime juice. Allow to simmer, then add slices of fish and heat through. Serve on toast.

EGG PLANT ELEGANTE (GARDEN EGG)

1 peeled egg plant   *   chopped garlic (1 clove)
2 boiled crushed potatoes   *   vinegar and oil
* salt, pepper, flour, oil

1. Slice garden egg lengthwise into fingers.
2. Season with salt and pepper and roll in flour.
3. Drop into deep hot oil and fry until crisp.
4. Combine crushed potatoes, garlic and enough vinegar and oil to make a paste of dipping consistency.
5. Place in a bowl and use fried egg plant fingers as scoops.

GRAPEFRUIT WITH SHRIMP AND SOUR CREAM

½ grapefruit per person
6 shrimp, cooked and cleaned
   per person

1 cup sour cream
1 tablespoon mayonnaise

1. Cut grapefruit in half. Core and remove pulp. Discard seeds.
2. Fill with cooked shrimp, marinated in sour cream and mayonnaise and mixed with grapefruit pulp.

PINEAPPLE APPETIZER

* pieces of fresh pineapple
* cream cheese

* chopped cashew nuts

1. Dip pieces of pineapple in cheese and roll in cashews.
2. Serve on toothpicks.

CURRIED ACKEES

24 ackees
1   cup coconut milk
½   teaspoon salt
½   teaspoon lime juice
1   teaspoon chutney or hot sauce

2   tablespoons flour
1   tablespoon curry powder
2   tablespoons butter or oil
1   onion
1   red pepper

1. Wash and prepare ackees for cooking - by discarding seeds and pink lining.
2. Cook for 5 minutes in boiling, salted water. Drain ackees and set aside.
3. Heat oil and add curry powder. Cook on slow heat.
4. Add all ingredients except ackees and bring to a boil. Skim.
5. Lower heat and cook until the taste of the curry has disappeared.
6. Add ackees, cook on a very gentle flame until the ackees are tender.
7. Serve on toasted rounds or breadcups.

BREAD CUPS

1. Remove crust from slices.
2. Use rolling pin to flatten slices.
3. Press into muffin pans to shape.
4. Bake at 350° for 10 minutes or until cups are firm and stay in shape.
5. Remove from muffin tin and allow to cool.
6. Fill cups just before serving.

COCONUT CHIPS

1   dry coconut   *   salt to taste

   1.   Remove meat from shell.
   2.   Cut meat into thin strips and arrange in a shallow pan.
   3.   Sprinkle with salt and toast in a slow oven. Turn occasionally.

FRIED PLANTAIN CHIPS

1   green plantain   *   oil

   1.   Peel plantain and cut into 1/6" thick slices.
   2.   Fry in hot oil. Drain on paper towel.
   3.   Sprinkle with salt to serve.

PORK RIND (SKIN)

*   whatever quantity desired   *   salt
2-3 tablespoons oil

   1.   Cut rind (skin) into small pieces and fry until crisp in oil.
   2.   Sprinkle with salt.

COCO FRITTERS

2   cocos   *   salt pepper
1   tablespoon flour   1   egg
1   teaspoon baking powder   *   oil
*   chopped escallion

   1.   Wash and peel cocos. Grate and mix with other ingredients.
   2.   Drop by spoonsful into hot oil.
   3.   When golden brown, remove and drain.

ACKEE WITH CHEESE

3   cups cooked ackees, crushed   1   tablespoon each butter, salt, pepper
2   cups mild grated cheese

Mix all together, heat through and serve on toast.

FRIED BAMMY

1   pkg. bammy (4 to a pkg)   ½   cup vegetable oil
½   cup milk   *   salt to taste

1. Cut bammies into quarters or wedges.
2. In a bowl, soak bammies in milk, 2 minutes per side. Remove and set aside.
3. In large saucepan over medium heat, fry bammy in oil until golden brown (You can also brush each side with margarine and grill.)
4. Place on paper towels to absorb excess oil. Sprinkle with salt before serving. Serve hot with fried fish.

PEPPER SHRIMPS

1   pint of shrimps - in shell   ½   onion sliced
*   white vinegar, water   2   cloves garlic
*   sliced hot pepper (remove the seeds)   *   salt and pimento grains

1. Rinse shrimp.
2. Cover shrimp with salted water and boil until tender.
3. Allow to cool.
4. Mix vinegar, peppers, onions, garlic and pimento grains. Bring to a boil.
5. Pour over shrimps and store in a covered jar for 12 hours before serving. Serves six.

RIO COBRE MUD

1   chopped onion   3   tablespoons grated cheese
1   tablespoon butter   *   creole sauce to taste
1   tin red pea soup   *   a drop of hot sauce

1. Fry onion in butter.
2. Add red pea soup and cheese. Stir over a low flame until cheese is melted.
3. Add sauces to taste and serve hot on slices of toast.

WATER MELON MARBLES

1   water melon   2   tablespoons sugar
¼   pint rum   *   cherries
2   oranges

1. Cut the melon in half lengthwise. Remove the seeds, then with a ball-scoop remove the flesh of the melon. The shell can be kept to be a serving dish if wished.
2. Place the melon balls in a bowl. Mix the rum, orange juice and sugar together, and pour over the melon balls. Refrigerate for at least one hour.
3. To serve, place a cocktail stick in each ball and pile up on a bed of cracked ice in the melon shell.

SEASONED BREADFRUIT CHIPS WITH AVOCADO CREAM CHEESE DIP

BREADFRUIT CHIPS

1	breadfruit	*	onion salt
*	salt	*	garlic powder
*	black pepper	*	oil

1. Peel breadfruit, cut into sections and remove the heart. Cut into slices and place in salted water for half an hour or more.
2. Dry the slices and fry in hot fat until golden. Drain on paper towels.
3. Meanwhile, mix the salt and seasonings together, and sprinkle over the chips just before serving.

AVOCADO CREAM CHEESE DIP

1	medium avocado pear	1	tablespoon lemon or lime juice
6	ozs. cream cheese	2	tablespoons milk
½	teaspoon minced onion	*	salt

1. Halve avocado lengthwise and remove seed.
2. Scoop out the pulp. The shell can be saved to be used as a container for serving, otherwise discard.
3. Mash the pulp with cream cheese and other ingredients. Serve piled in a small dish or the shell, surrounded by breadfruit chips.

STAMP AND GO (CODFISH FRITTERS)

¼	lb. salted codfish	¼	teaspoon hot pepper sauce or ¼ scotch bonnet pepper
*	lime juice		
¼	lb. flour	1	teaspoon baking powder
*	water	1	clove garlic
1	minced onion	2	tablespoon oil
1	diced tomato	1	stalk escallion

1. Wash codfish with lime juice, dry, and mince with onions and tomatoes. Add the flour and hot sauce with a little water to make a batter.
2. Heat oil in a skillet. Drop the mixture by the spoonful into the skillet and press down so that fritters are quite thin.
3. Fry on both sides until golden brown and crisp. Drain on paper towel and serve warm. Yields 12.

FRIED PLANTAIN

2	ripe plantains, peeled and sliced lengthwise or in circles	½	cup vegetable oil

1. In a large, heavy saucepan over medium heat, fry plantain on both sides until golden brown.
2. Remove plantain from pan and place on paper towels to absorb excess oil.

FESTIVAL

1	cup flour	3	tbsp. sugar
½	cup cornmeal	2	tbsp. milk
1	tbsp. baking powder	¾	cup water
¼	tsp. salt	1	cup vegetable oil

1. In a medium bowl, combine flour, cornmeal, baking powder, salt, and sugar. In a separate bowl, combine milk and water.
2. Make a well in the centre of the flour mixture, then pour in milk mixture. Using a spoon, mix well, then knead into a soft dough.
3. Cut into 12 equal pieces and roll lengthwise. In a deep-fat fryer or heavy saucepan, heat oil to 360°F.
4. Deep-fry pieces until golden brown. Drain on paper towels to remove excess oil. Serve hot.

CODFISH BALLS

1	lb. codfish	*	black pepper
1	lb. fresh pumpkin	*	salt
1	tablespoon butter, softened	2	cups fresh breadcrumbs
2	eggs	*	oil

1. Soak fish overnight. Discard water and cover with cold water. Bring to a boil and cook until tender. Skin, bone and flake finely.
2. Cook the pumpkin until tender. Mash thoroughly then beat in the softened butter, 2 lightly beaten eggs and pepper. Add salt to taste. The mixture should be firm enough to hold its shape. If not, beat in breadcrumbs as needed.
3. Shape the mixture into balls, dipping each in the breadcrumbs. Fry for about 3 to 4 minutes, turning regularly. When golden brown, drain on paper towels. Serve warm. A tomato sauce goes well with this dish.

STUFFED HARD-BOILED EGGS

4   hard boiled eggs

1. Boil eggs by putting in cold water. Boil for 15 minutes.
2. When boiled, remove from hot water and put in cold water to cool.
3. Break shells, remove eggs and rinse.
4. Cut boiled eggs into halves, lengthwise or crosswise, with a knife or crimp cutter.
5. Remove yolks, wash the white of the eggs. Drain and insert fillings in the centre,

2   tsp. mayonnaise   2   strips crisp fried bacon
2   tsp. grated cheese   4   ripe olives

1.   Mashed egg yolks & mayonnaise.
2.   Chopped ripe olives and cheese.
3.   Mashed egg yolks, mayonnaise, crisp bacon and cheese.

CORNMEAL FRITTERS

4   ozs. cornmeal   10 ozs. milk
1   tin whole kernel   1   teaspoon salt
2   ozs. flour   *   oil for frying
1   egg

1.   Mix together cornmeal, flour, egg, milk and salt.
2.   Add tin of whole kernel corn and stir.
3.   Pour oil into frying pan and allow it to become very hot.
4.   Drop the mixture (with a teaspoon) into the hot oil and fry until golden brown on
     each side.
5.   Allow each fritter to drain on paper towel.

Soup

MANNISH WATER

4	lbs. goat head, feet and tripe	2	lbs. yam
1	2 green bananas	3	gallons water
1	lb. flour	½	lb. escallion
2	hot peppers (scotch bonnet)	4	sprigs thyme
½	lb. carrot	*	salt to taste
2	chochos		

1. Chop meat into small pieces.
2. Wash and place in a large stock pot.
3. Boil for approximately 2 hrs. or until meat is cooked soft.
4. Peel bananas and cut into small pieces along with the yam. Dice all other vegetable ingredients.
5. Cook uncovered for approximately one more hour.
6. Use flour to make "spinners" (small dumplings). Add to soup.
7. Add more water (if necessary) and seasoning to taste. Serve hot.

CHOCHO PUREE

4	chochos peeled and diced	*	butter, herbs, salt, nutmeg to taste
1	cup milk		

1. Boil chocho until tender. Pour into blender with herbs and milk and blend until smooth.
2. Reheat to serve with a dab of butter and pinch of nutmeg.

COCO SOUP

4	cocos	2	slices of bacon
1	lb. soup meat	1	tablespoon butter
2	qrts. water		

1. Chop up cocos and place in a pot with water and soup meat and bacon.
2. Boil until cocos are soft and meat is cooked.
3. Remove meat, put cocos and liquid through a blender or sieve.
4. Season to taste. Add the meat and a dab of margarine. Reheat to serve.

CREAM OF PUMPKIN SOUP

3	cups boiled pureed pumpkin (1½ lbs)	2	tablespoons butter/ margarine
3	tablespoons flour	1	teaspoon granulated sugar
2	cups milk	*	salt and black pepper to taste
1	onion chopped	*	3 teaspoons sherry

1. In a saucepan, melt butter and fry onions.
2. Add flour, salt, pepper and sugar and cook well.
3. Add milk slowly, stirring blending butter, flour and milk mixture. Add sherry to mixture.
4. Combine pumpkin with mixture. Stir until smooth and thickened.
5. Simmer for five minutes. Serves 6.

COLD THICK CUCUMBER SOUP

½	cup diced cucumber	1	cup milk
¾	cup diced cooked chicken	2	tablespoons sour cream
1	cup diced and cooked lobster meat	*	salt, pepper, parsley
¼	cup chopped onion		

1. Mix the milk into the sour cream and thin down.
2. Add all other ingredients. Chill for 2 hours before serving.

GOAT HEAD SOUP

1	goat head	12	small dumplings
1	lb. pumpkin	1	chopped onion
1	lb. carrots	*	herbs, salt, pepper and a small
1	chocho		piece of crushed ginger root.
6	green bananas	3	qrts. water
1	lb. yellow yam		

1. Prepare and clean goat's head. Put to boil in a large soup pot with water. Skim.
2. When meat is tender, remove bones and put flesh back into liquid. Keep boiling.
3. Prepare and add the vegetables, seasoning and peppers. Soup must be of thick consistency.

CHICKEN SOUP

4	lbs. chicken	2	sliced potatoes
2	qrts. water	*	onion, thyme, salt and a hot pepper
2	sliced carrots		

1. Boil the chicken in water. When tender, strain and skim. Add vegetables, seasonings, and strips of meat to the liquid.
2. Boil until vegetables are tender. Water may be added if it has boiled away.
3. Remove the hot pepper without breaking it in the cooking liquid.

BEET SOUP

8	large cooked and peeled beets	1	cup shredded cabbage
1	lb. soup meat cut into cubes	*	salt, pepper
3	diced tomatoes	*	sour cream
2	qrts. water		

1. Combine meat, tomatoes and water in a saucepan. Bring to a boil. Skim and cook for about an hour.
2. Add the cabbage, salt, and pepper. Cook for 30 minutes.
3. Grate the beetroots and add to the soup with salt and pepper.
4. Cook for 15 minutes.
5. Serve very hot, with a spoonful of sour cream and a few pieces of the meat in each soup bowl.

COW HEEL SOUP

1	pair of cow heels	1	chopped coco
6	cups water	1	hot pepper
1	chopped onion	2	teaspoons salt
1	diced chocho	*	squeeze of lime juice
1	diced carrot	*	parsley

1. Wash cow heels in lime juice. Cut up and boil in salted water. Skim frequently. Cook 2-3 hours over low heat.
2. Add vegetables and seasonings.
3. Boil until vegetables are tender. Serve with chopped parsley.

FISH CHOWDER

2	lbs. of any type of white fish meat	1	diced potato
1	qrt. water	2	diced tomatoes
1	minced onion	*	salt and pepper to taste
2	diced carrots	*	sherry, optional

1. Boil fish in water until tender. Remove all bones and strain the liquid.
2. Stir diced vegetables into fish stock with seasonings. When cooked add some flaked fish meat and sherry to taste.

JAMAICA FISH TEA

3	lbs. of fish cut into pieces	1	hot pepper
6	cups water	1	tsp. thyme
2	chopped onions	*	squeeze of lime juice
2	chopped tomatoes		

1. Place all ingredients in a pot with water.
2. Bring to a boil and simmer gently for about an hour.
3. Strain off liquid and serve with chopped parsley.

GUNGO OR COW PEA SOUP

1 pint of peas (soaked overnight)	* flour (for spinners)
2 qrts. water	1 chopped onion
1 lb. soup meat	* thyme, salt, pepper, pepper, escallion
½ lb. pig's tail or salted beef	
1 sliced coco	

1. Cut up and soak salted meat in water to remove excess salt.
2. Boil peas with soup meat and pigstail in water until tender.
3. Remove the meat and put peas through a colander, rub out and discard skin.
4. Place liquid on stove with seasonings and coco.
5. Add more water if necessary. When coco is cooked and dissolved, the soup is ready. Bits of the boiled meat can be added.

PAW PAW (PAPAYA) SOUP - NIGERIA

2 tablespoons butter	* a sprig of parsley
1 sliced onion	* salt, pepper and a dash of nutmeg
1 paw paw peeled, seeded and sliced	3 cups milk
- use a fruit which is past the	1 tablespoon cornstarch
green stage but not yet ripe	3 cups water

1. Melt butter and fry onions. Add the paw paw, water, parsley, salt and pepper. Cover boil over a low heat for about one hour, or until paw paw is tender enough to force through a sieve.
2. Return to saucepan and add nutmeg. Mix cornstarch into milk until smooth, and add to the paw paw mixture. Stir constantly.
3. Cook for 10 minutes more over low heat but do not allow to boil.

JAMAICAN PEPPER POT

2 lbs. of chopped callaloo or spinach	½ lb. beef stew
2 qrts. Water	Yellow Yam
½ of a pig's tail	1 lb. pre-cooked shrimp
¼ lb. flour	1 doz. okras sliced
2 stalks escallion	1 minced onion
1 clove garlic	1 coco
1 scotch bonnet pepper	* salt, pepper, herbs, hot pepper to taste
¼ lb. salt beef	

1. Cut salted beef and pig's tail into small pieces. Soak to get rid of excess salt.
2. Cut beefstew into chunks.
3. Boil both beef and pig's tail until cooked soft (you may cook them in a pressure cooker).
4. Wash callaloo or spinach and add to water. Cook for approximately 10 minutes. Remove from stock and puree in a blender or food processor.
5. Cut up okras, peel yam and cocoa and cut into small pieces.
6. Add okras, yam, coco, green pepper and garlic to water.
7. Make spinners.
8. Add to stock along with pureed callaloo.
9. Simmer for approximately 30 minutes or until soup is thickened.
10. Add escallion, thyme and cook for approximately fifteen minutes.
11. Add shrimp and cook for five minutes. Serve hot.

RED PEA SOUP

1	pint of red peas (soak overnight)	1	sliced coco
2	qrts. water	1	minced onion
1	lb. soup meat	*	salt, thyme, hot pepper to taste
¼	lb. of pig's tail		

1. Place peas and meats in water. Boil until peas are almost tender. Add coco and seasonings. When peas and coco are cooked, remove the meats.
2. Soup may be served with whole peas, or, put through a colander and discard skins. Small dumplings are usually added to this soup.

TRIPE SOUP

4	lbs. tripe	2	diced potatoes
½	cup vinegar	2	cups diced chochos
1	pair pig's trotters	*	salt and pepper
2	chopped onions	4	qrts. water

1. Soak tripe and trotters in vinegar with water to cover for 2 hours. Drain and rinse.
2. Place tripe, trotters and 4 qrts. of water into a pot. Bring to a boil and skim.
3. Cook over a low heat for about 3 hours.
4. Strain off the liquid. Cut tripe into small pieces and set aside. Discard trotters.
5. Using about 6 cups of the liquid, add seasonings and vegetables.
6. Cook for about ½ hour. Add the tripe and simmer for a further ten minutes. Season to taste. This is a thick soup.

Fish & Shellfish

ACKEE AND SALTFISH

1 lb. codfish	1 large onion
24 ackees	1 medium tomato
2 ozs. fried bacon	¼ of a sweet pepper
4 ozs. margarine or two tablespoons oil	* scotch bonnet pepper to taste
2 tablespoons margarine or butter	

1. Soak fish overnight and discard the water. Cover with cold water and boil until tender.
2. Skin, debone and flake, and set aside.
3. Prepare ackees removing seed and pink lining.
4. Boil quickly until soft but whole.
5. In a separate pan, add oil or melt margarine, sauté onions tomatoes and pepper.
6. Simmer a few minutes, then add the bacon, fish and ackees. Simmer for two minutes.

BAKED STUFFED CALAPEEVA (FOUND IN JAMAICAN RIVERS)

6 calapeeva	2 sliced onions
1 cup breadcrumbs	1 tablespoon rum
* parsley, salt, pepper to taste	1 tablespoon oil
1 dessertspoon butter	

1. Wash and clean fish with lime juice.
2. Make a stuffing of breadcrumbs, parsley, salt and pepper, moistened with a little melted butter.
3. Stuff the fish and place on a bed of sliced onions, which have been slightly sautéed in hot oil. Add 1 tablespoon rum and cover with some bread crumbs.
4. Bake in a moderate oven until fish are tender.

BANANA KING FISH WITH MUSTARD SAUCE

4	king fish steaks	*	salt
2	ripe bananas	*	pepper
4	slices Cheddar cheese	*	butter

1. Season the fish steaks with salt and pepper. Fry gently in butter.
2. Place the steaks in a heat-proof dish.
3. Cover each steak with slices of ripe banana and top with a slice of cheddar cheese.
4. Broil until the cheese is melted and the banana heated through. Serve with mustard sauce.

Mustard Sauce

4	tablespoons mayonnaise	1	teaspoon lime juice
4	tablespoons vinegar	3	teaspoons dry mustard
4	tablespoons salad oil	*	salt and pepper to taste

Mix all ingredients until smooth.

BAKED BLACK CRABS

6	Black Crabs, boiled	1	teaspoon vinegar
1	oz. butter, softened	*	salt
½	teaspoon black pepper	*	breadcrumbs
1	tablespoon chopped onion	*	butter
1	country pepper, finely chopped		

1. Clean the crabs and pick out all the meat, including the claws and smaller bones. Save four shells.
2. Mix the crab meat with the butter, onion, pepper, salt and vinegar. The mixture should be moist but not soggy.
3. Wash the shells well and wipe with a little oil. Fill each with the crab mixture, top with the breadcrumbs and dot with butter. Bake in a hot oven until the crumbs are brown.

CODFISH TWICE LAID

1	lb. codfish	2	tablespoons margarine or butter
1	lb. potatoes, boiled & sliced	*	breadcrumbs
1	sliced onion	*	pepper to taste

1. Soak fish overnight. Discard water and cover with cold water. Bring to a boil and cook until tender. Skin, bone and flake.
2. Fry onion lightly and add to the fish. In a casserole dish, place alternate layers of potatoes with fish-onion mixture.
3. Dot layers with butter and cover with breadcrumbs before baking until golden brown in a moderate oven.

CRAB FRITTERS

½ lb. cooked crab meat (use local   3   eggs
   black crabs)   1   tablespoon minced parsley
2   tablespoons oil   *   breadcrumbs, salt, pepper to taste
1   tablespoon chopped onion

1.   Add onion, seasoning and beaten egg to crab meat.
2.   Add enough breadcrumbs to bind mixture. Shape into fritters and fry lightly.

ESCOVEITCH OF FISH (GROUPER)

*   small fish or slices of king fish   2   tablespoons water
*   oil   1   chopped hot pepper
1   cup vinegar   *   a pimento leaf and a pinch of salt
2   sliced onions

1.   Fry fish in hot oil and set aside. Mix remaining ingredients together and bring to
      a boil. Simmer for about 20 minutes.
2.   Lay fish in a shallow dish. Cover with hot vinegar sauce and marinate for about 12
      hours before serving.

(In Mexico the fish is not cooked, it is marinated and eaten raw.)

FISH KEDEGEREE

1   cup cooked rice   1   cup cooked fish, tuna, salmon or
*   curry powder   codfish
*   mushrooms, optional   *   salt
*   lime rind   3   hard-boiled eggs

1.   Toss together cooked rice and flaked, cooked fish.
2.   Add a pinch of curry powder and some chopped mushrooms if available, a pinch
      of salt and a sprinkle of lime rind.
3.   Pack into a mould and bake for 30 minutes. Serve with chopped hard boiled eggs.

JAMAICA FISH PIE

2   cups cooked flaked fish   1   cup cooked, mashed potatoes
1   cup white sauce   1   cup flour
1   cup cooked peeled shrimps   *   pinch of salt
*   salt, pepper, chopped parsley   1   beaten egg

1.   Mix together fish, white sauce, shrimp, seasonings and parsley and place in a
      deep pie dish.
2.   Mix remaining ingredients to form a dough. Roll out on a floured board and cut to
      cover pie. Place dough over fish mixture and prick top with a fork.
3.   Bake in a moderate oven about 30 minutes or till crust is brown.

BAKED GRUNTS

6   grunts
*   juice of 2 limes
*   water, hot pepper, salt

3   tablespoons butter
*   avocado slices

1.   Clean grunts, place in a greased dish and add lime juice and water to cover. Add salt and pieces of hot pepper.
2.   Cover and bake in a 350°F oven for about 20 minutes.
3.   Spread melted butter over them and serve with avocado slices.

KING FISH IN COCONUT CREAM

2   lbs. fish steaks
3   ozs. butter or margarine
1   cup coconut cream

*   salt, pepper
*   lime slices

1.   Heat butter and fry steaks until brown on both sides.
2.   To make coconut cream, grate a coconut, add water, squeeze and strain out cream, and discard pulp.
3.   Add to fish steaks with salt and pepper.
4.   Simmer for about 3 minutes. Garnish with lime slices.

KING FISH FILLETS

4   fillets of king fish
1   glass white wine
1   cup cooked and peeled shrimps
1   cup white sauce
1   egg

*   a pinch of salt and pepper
*   a squeeze of lime juice
2   tablespoons tomato sauce
1   cup breadcrumbs
2-3 tablespoons margarine or oil

1.   Soak fillets in white wine, salt, pepper, and lime juice for 1 hour. Pat dry. Make 1 cup of white sauce and add the cooked shrimps.
2.   When this is cool, spoon some of the mixture onto each fish and roll up.
3.   Dip in breadcrumbs, then into beaten egg and again in crumbs. Fry in hot oil. Serve with tomato sauce.

LOBSTER CREOLE

2   lbs. cooked and shredded lobster meat
*   chopped onions
*   chopped sweet peppers
3   diced tomatoes

2   tablespoons rum or sherry
4   tablespoons oil
*   salt, pepper, to taste

1.   Fry onion and peppers until tender. Stir in salt and pepper. Add tomatoes and simmer gently. Add lobster meat with rum or sherry.
2.   Continue to simmer gently for about 10 minutes. Serve with plain boiled rice.

MACKEREL ALOHA

1   tin drained mackerel
½   cup diced pineapple
2   tablespoons chopped peanuts

¼   cup mayonnaise
1   tablespoon lime juice

1. Break up mackerel.
2. Combine with remaining ingredients and toss.
3. Serve in shells or lettuce cups. Sardines can also be served in this manner.

OCTOPUS (called "Sea Puss" by local fishermen)

1   small octopus
3   tablespoons butter

*   salted water to cover

1. Cut octopus into small pieces and place in a pot of salted water.
2. Bring to a boil and cook until octopus is tender.
3. Drain, dry and fry in butter. Serve with one of the following sauces.

PIQUANT SAUCE

1   tablespoon oil
2   tablespoons vinegar

½   chopped onion
*   pinch salt and pepper

Mix all ingredients together.

CHEESE SAUCE

6   tablespoons flour
6   tablespoons margarine
2   cups milk

1   cup grated cheese
*   salt to taste

1. Melt margarine and blend in flour and milk. Stir constantly until thick.
2. Add cheese and salt. Heat until cheese is melted.

SHRIMP WITH PINEAPPLE

24 large shrimp, cleaned, peeled
    and cooked
1   tablespoon cornflour
½   pint pineapple juice
2   tablespoons soya sauce

1   tablespoon honey
1   tablespoon vinegar
¼   teaspoon ginger powder
1   small tin of pineapple chunks

1. Blend cornflour with a little of the pineapple juice.
2. Combine with remaining juice, soya sauce, honey, vinegar and ginger.
3. Cook over a low heat, stirring until thickened.
4. Thread shrimps and pineapple chunks alternately on to skewers and dip into sauce. Grill until slightly golden in colour.

RED STRIPE BATTER FOR FISH

¼ cup cornstarch
¼ cup flour
¼ cup beer (Red Stripe)

2   egg whites
¼ cup margarine or oil
*   salt to taste

Any type of fish may be used.
1. Mix cornstarch and flour and salt. Add beer and beat until smooth.
2. Beat egg whites and fold into batter.
3. Dip slices of fish or whole small fish into this batter and fry in bubbling fat.

Poultry

DRUNK CHICKEN

2 lbs. chicken cut in pieces	1 teaspoon salt
2 qrts. water	* sherry or rum or white wine

1. Heat to boiling 2 qrts. of water, salt and chicken; cover and simmer for about 15 minutes.
2. Place chicken in a bowl or jar and cover completely with liquor.
3. Keep refrigerated for one week. Serve cold.

CHICKEN WITH LIME AND OLIVES

2½ lbs. chicken	1½ cups water
¼ cup oil	1 tablespoon lime juice
1½ cups minced onions	2 doz. small pitted olives
½ teaspoon powdered ginger	* salt, pepper

1. Cut chicken into pieces and brown on all sides in oil.
2. Remove chicken and fry onions. Stir in ginger, salt and pepper and simmer for 2 minutes.
3. Add water, lime juice and chicken pieces.
4. Simmer for 30 minutes. Add olives a few minutes before serving.

TROPICAL CHICKEN

4 young coconuts	1 diced onion
1 small chicken	½ cup corn kernels
2 cups chicken broth	3 tablespoons curry powder
1 cup rice	* salt, pepper
1 cup chopped pineapple	

1. Slice off top of coconuts and take a thin slice off the bottoms also, so that the coconut will stand upright. Pour off water and reserve.
2. Steam chicken in coconut water. When tender, remove, cool and shred the meat.
3. Steam rice in 2 cups of broth (adding water if needed). Mix in pineapple, onions, corn and curry powder. Season to taste.
4. Stuff coconuts with this mixture, placing alternate layers with the shredded chicken. Replace tops on coconut and sit in a shallow pan of water.
5. Bake in a moderate oven for one hour. If water in pan evaporates, add more.

A DIFFERENT STUFFING FOR ROASTED CHICKEN

1   cup cooked rice
½   cup raisins
¼   cup finely chopped onions

*   diced cooked chicken liver
2   ozs. butter
1   egg

1. Mash the chicken livers and mix all ingredients together, working the butter well into mixture.
2. Add the beaten egg last to bind.

ROAST CHICKEN WITH RICE STUFFING

3-4 lbs. whole chicken
½   teaspoon salt
2   cloves garlic

1   teaspoon black pepper
1   sprig thyme
½   teaspoon poultry

RICE STUFFING
1   cup boiled rice
1   small onion

1   stalk celery

1. Rinse chicken in lime water and drain.
2. Cut up garlic, scallion, thyme very fine and season with salt, black pepper and place in cavity.
3. Rub over chicken and marinate for one hour.
4. Shake off chicken.
5. Prepare stuffing by mixing all ingredients.
6. Place stuffing lightly in neck cavity.
7. Pull neck skin over stuffing and fasten with skewer.
8. Stuff body cavity skewers or needle & thread and draw body together.
9. Cross legs off the bird, wind cord around and draw tightly. Then tie around the parson's nose.
10. Place on a rack, breast up, in a shallow roasting pan.
11. Brush all over continuously with melted butter or margarine.
12. Roast at 180°C/350°F at 15 minutes to the pound or until done.
13. Droppings from pan may be used to make gravy after baking. Serves 6-8 persons.

GUINEA HEN AFRICAN STYLE

½   butter or margarine
2   small guinea hens cut into pieces
1   minced onion
1   tablespoon flour
1   cup water

3   chopped tomatoes
3   sweet potatoes, cubed
5   firm ripe plantains, sliced
*   salt, pepper

1. Melt all but 3 tablespoons butter in a large pot or casserole.
2. Add the guinea hen pieces, onions, some salt and pepper and sauté in some of the butter.
3. Sprinkle with flour and add water and tomatoes.
4. Cook over low heat for 25 minutes. Add sweet potato cubes and cook until tender. Season to taste.
5. Melt remaining butter and fry plantain slices. Skim all fat from gravy and serve plantain slices separately.

BRAISED GUINEA HEN

1 prepared guinea hen
* fat
1 lump of butter
1 lb. carrots

1 clove garlic
1 sliced onion
* parsley, thyme, salt, pepper to taste

1. Put butter inside guinea hen and brown in sizzling fat.
2. Clean and slice carrots lengthwise and add to pan with garlic, onion and herbs.
3. Cover and cook about an hour depending on the age of the bird. Wine may be added to the sauce.

GUINEA FOWL STEW

1 guinea fowl
4 onions
2 tomatoes
2 hard boiled eggs
2 cups crushed peanuts

1 cup water
2 cloves garlic
½ teaspoon salt
* oil
* boiled white rice

1. Put peanuts into 1 cup water and boil for 12 minutes until the peanut oil shows on the side of the pot.
2. Cut up guinea fowl and sauté in oil. Add diced tomatoes, onions and garlic.
3. Finally, add all the peanuts and seasoning. Mix well and fry for 5 minutes.
4. Empty into a pot adding more water if needed and stew until flesh is tender.
5. When cooked, float halved hard boiled eggs on the top and serve with boiled white rice.

PIGEONS WITH CABBAGE

2 pigeons
1 small cabbage
1 onion
2 pieces bacon
½ cup water

* juice of 1 lime
½ cup raisins
* a pinch of salt
* sugar and pepper to taste

1. Cut the birds in half down the backbone. Melt fat from bacon and fry the birds in this. Remove birds.
2. Slice onion and sauté in the same pan. Add sugar and raisins. Shred cabbage and add to the pan. Stir to coat.
3. Heat water and lime juice and add to pan with a sprinkle of salt.
4. Place the pieces of pigeons on top of the cabbage. Cover and simmer for about 1 hour.
5. Season to taste.

PIGEON PIE

3	pigeons cut into pieces		*	diced ham
*	salt and pepper		2	cups chicken broth
3	tablespoons oil			

1. Season pigeons with salt and pepper and fry in oil. Add diced ham and stock. Place in a deep pie dish and cover with crust.
2. Bake in 350° oven 30 minutes or till crust is lightly browned.

PIE CRUST

1	cup flour	2-3	tablespoons cold water
4	ozs. butter, margarine or shortening	*	pinch of salt

1. Sift together flour and salt.
2. Mix fat into flour by using 2 knives and "cutting" in the fat till it is pea-sized and coated with flour.
3. Sprinkle water over flour using a minimum amount to moisten mixture. Shape mixture into a mound and roll out.
4. Cut to fit dish.

PIGEONS WITH PINEAPPLE

½	of a ripe pineapple	4	tablespoons brandy or rum if preferred
4	squabs (young pigeons)		
¼	cup butter	*	salt, pepper to taste
¼	cup paté	½	cup pineapple juice

1. Peel, slice and dice pineapple. Wash and dry squabs. Into each body cavity put 1 tablespoon paté and a piece of pineapple. Close cavity and rub squabs with salt and pepper.
2. Melt ½ of the butter in a heavy casserole dish and brown the squabs. Do not prick the skins.
3. Flame with 1 tablespoon brandy or rum (heat, ignite and pour over squabs). Pour in the remaining butter, and roast squabs in 350°F oven uncovered, basting often, for about 45 minutes.
4. While squabs are roasting, poach slices of pineapple in the rest of liquor for 10 minutes.
5. Arrange slices on the squabs to serve.

BALDPATE SPATCHCOCK

3	baldpate doves	1	teaspoon pepper
2	tablespoons melted butter	*	juice of a lime
1	teaspoon salt	*	fat for basting

1. Prepare doves, wash with lime juice and season.
2. Split through the backbone and flatten the birds. Wipe dry.
3. Bake in hot oven basting frequently for about 15 minutes.
4. Remove from the oven, place under a grill, dribble melted butter over the birds and grill on both sides.

WHITE WING OR ANY OTHER DOVE WITH CREAM

4	doves	¼	pint cream (or evaporated milk)
4	slices bacon	*	a few black olives
4	tablespoons butter	*	salt and pepper to taste

1. Cover the breast of each bird with a slice of bacon and season. Place 1 tablespoon butter inside each.
2. Roast in a hot 400-450°F oven for 30 minutes.
3. Remove birds, drain off surplus fat and add cream to the pan.
4. Simmer slowly and season to taste. Add olives, and pour over the birds.

BRAISED DUCKLING

13½ -4 lb. duckling		1	cup chicken stock
4	ozs. butter	½	lb. young sliced turnips
2	onions	2	ozs. Butter
2	carrots	*	salt, pepper to taste
¼	cup brandy or wine		

1. Brown duck on all sides in a casserole dish. Put in the onions and sliced carrots, browning them also.
2. Pour in the liquor and all the stock with salt and pepper. Place in a moderate oven 350° and baste frequently.
3. When duck is ready, keep it warm.
4. Strain the liquid, remove vegetables and reduce the sauce. Serve with the young turnips which have been cooked whilst duck was braising.
5. Blanch the turnips first, then sauté in butter.

SALMI OF DUCK

1	duck	1½ pints chicken stock (chicken cubes melted in water)
2	ozs. butter	
1	oz. flour	* salt, pepper
1	onion, chopped	* brandy or wine

1. Roast duck, cook till slightly underdone. Cut into neat joints.
2. Melt 1 oz. butter and fry onion. Add stock, simmer for 1 hour and strain.
3. Melt remaining butter, stir in flour and add the stock. Season and simmer 15 minutes.
4. Add the pieces of duck and cook 20 minutes longer. Brandy or wine is usually added to taste.

DUCK AND PINEAPPLE

1	4 lb. duck	½	cup water	
1	tin pineapple slices	2	tablespoons sugar	
2	tablespoons oil	*	a pinch of salt	
1	tablespoon rum			

1. Clean and roast the duck. Cool, remove bones and slice. Drain pineapple slices and dice.
2. Place duck and pineapple in alternate layers in a casserole dish.
3. Add the pineapple juice mixed with oil soya sauce, rum, water, sugar and salt.
4. Bake in moderate oven for 1 hour. Serve with rice and green salad.

TEAL WITH ORANGE SAUCE

*	teal (wild duck)	*	oil
*	salt and pepper		

1. Prepare and season birds.
2. Roast till done, in a moderate oven, basting with cooking fats and adding a little oil if necessary.

SAUCE

*	juice of 2 oranges	1	tablespoon rum
*	2 cloves	*	orange segments
1	dessertspoon cornstarch		

1. Mix juice with cloves and thicken with cornstarch moistened first in some of the juice.
2. Add rum and orange juice to liquid and boil very slowly to thicken in a double boiler. Serve over teal.

CURRIED GOAT

2 lbs. goat	1 tablespoon lime juice
1 lb. irish potato	1 tablespoon butter
2 tablespoons curry powder	2 cloves garlic
2 sliced onions	1 stalk escallion
2 cups hot water	* salt, oil

1. Cut meat into bite-size pieces.
2. Season with curry powder, escallion, garlic, pepper and salt and set aside for at least one hour.
3. Remove seasoning from meat and set aside.
4. Brown meat in hot oil.
5. Add 2 cups of hot water and onions.
6. Cook slowly until tender, adding more water, butter, lime juice & curry powder if necessary, stirring to prevent burning.
7. Simmer until cooked (approximately 2 hrs.).
8. Serve with plain boiled rice and side dishes of nuts, grated coconut, mango chutney, sliced onions soaked in hot sauce and slices of fried ripe plantain. Serves 4-6.

STEWED OXTAIL

2½ lbs. oxtails, cut into ½" pieces	2 tbsp. fresh thyme, chopped
1 tbsp. salt	1½ cups water
1 tbsp. black pepper	2 tbsp. soy sauce
½ tsp. paprika	2 tbsp. ketchup
3 tbsp. vegetable oil	¼ tsp. jerk sauce (optional)
3 cloves garlic, chopped	1 14oz. can lima beans
1 large onion, chopped	10-12 spinners (optional)

1. In a large bowl, season oxtail with salt, pepper, and paprika.
2. In a large saucepan over medium heat, brown oxtails in oil for 15 minutes. Add garlic, onion, and thyme and sauté for another 2 minutes.
3. Lower heat, add ½ cup water, cover and let simmer for 45 minutes to 1 hour, stirring often and adding remaining water when needed.
4. Stir in remaining ingredients and cook another 10 minutes.

BEEF AND MANGO IN BEER

12 ozs. minced beef
1 cup Red Stripe Beer
1 cup water
½ cup mango chutney

* pinch of salt and onion powder
1 dessertspoon soy sauce
½ cup rice
1 cup green peas

1. Combine beef, beer, water, chutney, onions, powder, salt and soy sauce in a casserole and bake in oven for 1 hour at 350°F.
2. Add rice and cook for ½ hour. Just before serving, add the peas.

SALTED BEEF AND BANANA CASSEROLE

½ lb. diced, cooked, salted beef
2 eggs
1 cup grated cheese

½ cup milk
1 cup diced ripe bananas
* salt, pepper, marjoram

1. Beat eggs, stir in cheese, beef, milk, pepper, marjoram and bananas.
2. Use very little salt if any. Turn into a casserole and bake for about 40 minutes in a 350°F oven.

DUMPERPUMPKIN

1 small pumpkin
2 cups prepared sweet and sour beef

½ cup seeded prunes

1. Wash pumpkin and place in a large pot.
2. Cover with water and bring to a boil.
3. When cooked, but not soft, remove, cut off the top and scoop out seeds and core.
4. Fill with sweet and sour beef mix and prunes. Refit top.
5. Place pumpkin in a baking dish with water and bake for 30-40 minutes in a moderate oven - add more water if necessary.

SWEET AND SOUR BEEF FILLING

2 lbs. steak, cubed
* fat or oil
1 tablespoon sugar
1 cup water
3 tablespoons vinegar

1 teaspoon soya sauce
1 teaspoon tomato ketchup
* pinch of salt and ginger powder
1 dessertspoon cornstarch

1. Fry steak in oil and cook through. In a separate pot, bring next six ingredients to a boil and thicken with a little cornstarch blended in some water.
2. Pour over the cubed steak. Simmer for about ½ hour.
3. Fill pumpkin cavity and transfer to oven for 30 mins.

26

STEWED COW'S FOOT

3	lbs. cow's foot, sliced	½	tsp. Worcestershire sauce
6	cups water	3	tbsp. olive oil
2	cloves garlic, chopped	2	tbsp. soy sauce
6	whole cloves	1	tsp. onion powder
6	whole pimento (allspice) berries	1	tbsp. black pepper
1	tbsp. salt	½	tsp. ketchup
1	tbsp. black pepper	1	tsp. jerk sauce
2	medium onions, chopped	3	springs fresh thyme, chopped
2	springs fresh thyme, chopped	24	spinners
2	stalks escallion, chopped		

1. Wash cow's foot and, with a stiff brush, remove any hairs or rough spots.
2. In a large saucepan over medium heat, combine cow's foot, water, garlic, cloves, allspice, salt, and pepper.
3. Cover and let simmer for 1½ hours until cow's foot is tender.
4. Add all remaining ingredients.
5. Lower heat, cover and let simmer another 15 minutes.

BEEF CURRY WITH GREEN BANANAS

3	peeled green bananas cut in ¼" slices	1½	tablespoons flour
1½	lbs. stewing beef	½	cup tomato ketchup
3	tablespoons oil	½	teaspoon salt
2	tablespoons curry powder	½	cup rum
2	onions		

1. Boil bananas in salted water for 20 minutes. Drain and reserve.
2. Cut beef into cubes and brown in oil. Transfer to a saucepan.
3. Add sliced onions. Stir in flour, salt and tomato ketchup and cook for 5 minutes.
4. Cover with curry powder mixed in some water. Stir and simmer for 1½ hrs. Add rum and green banana slices. Heat through.

RUMP STEAK CASSEROLE

2	lbs. steak	1	cup vinegar
¼	lb. margarine	*	salt, pepper, nutmeg and ginger to taste
1	dessertspoon sugar		
1	cup beef stock (tin of beef bouillon or consommé)	1	teaspoon marjoram
		*	chopped tomatoes, optional

1. Cut steaks into cubes and marinate for 2 hours in sugar, vinegar, seasoning and herbs.
2. Melt margarine and brown beef cubes. Moisten with some of the marinade.
3. Place meat in a casserole with 1 cup of beef stock.
4. Cover and bake in a 350°F oven until tender.
5. Skim off fat and add a few chopped tomatoes if desired.

POOR MAN'S FILLET

3   lbs. rib eye steak
2   tablespoons butter

*   bread slices

1.   Cut the steak allowing one slice per person.
2.   Rub with salt, pepper and garlic. Brown steak slices in hot butter. Fry slices of bread in butter.
3.   Slip a slice of steak onto each slice of bread and serve with sauce from frying pan.
4.   Takes about 3 minutes to prepare.

DEBONED STUFFED LEG OF KID

1   deboned leg of goat kid
1   cup breadcrumbs

*   milk

1.   Season meat with salt and pepper. Moisten breadcrumbs with milk and press dry.
2.   Add egg yolk, chopped parsley, salt and pepper to make a stuffing for meat.
3.   Fill, roll, and tie meat and bake for 1½ hours in a 350°F oven. Serve with baby carrots and small boiled onions.

MUTTON STEW (In Jamaica, goat meat is often referred to as mutton)

3   lbs. goat meat
1   teaspoon hot sauce
1   cup chopped onions
*   oil, salt, flour
1   cup sliced carrots

1   cup chopped tomatoes
1   cup sliced potatoes
4   cups hot water
*   some small flour dumplings

1.   Dredge cubed meat with flour and salt and brown in hot oil. Add water and simmer until meat is tender.
2.   Add sauce, onions, and vegetables. Cook until vegetables are ready. This process should take about 2 hours.
3.   When all is ready add the dumplings which will cook very quickly. Add more liquid if necessary.

LIVER WITH SWEET PEPPERS

1   lb. liver sliced thin
4   sweet peppers
1   teaspoon lime juice

1   tablespoon rum
½   cup oil
*   salt, pepper, a little flour

1.   Prepare sweet peppers by coring and removing seeds.
2.   Wash and cut into strips. Season liver with salt, pepper and lime juice.
3.   Dust with flour and sauté quickly in hot oil.
4.   Pour the rum over liver. Add the slices of pepper and cook gently for 15-20 minutes.

PORK CHOPS WITH GINGER ALE

4	chops		*	parsley
*	fat, salt, pepper		*	ginger ale

1. Brown chops lightly in fat. Add seasoning.
2. Place in individual squares of foil.
3. Sprinkle liberally with ginger ale. Fold squares tightly.
4. Place in a baking dish and bake in a 350°F oven for about 1½ hours.

MARINATED PORK CHOPS

4	chops		*	lime juice
*	salt, pepper		*	garlic powder

1. Sprinkle the chops with seasonings and lime juice and marinate for 2 hours.
2. Grill the chops and serve with a green salad. Instead of a dressing, pour the juices from the grilling pan.

SPARE RIBS

4	lbs. spare ribs		2	tablespoons soy sauce
2	tablespoons sugar		2	teaspoons oil
3	cloves garlic			salt to taste
3	stalks escallion		½	cup cornstarch

1. Boil spare ribs with salt for approximately 1½ -2hrs. or until tender.
2. Cool and cut in single ribs (or remain in rack).
3. Combine sugar, escallion, soy sauce, ketchup and garlic for marinade. Allow ribs to marinate for 2-3 hours.
4. Remove ribs and place in a baking pan. Add water and cornstarch to marinade and boil until thickened.
5. Brush ribs with marinade and place in oven at 350°F/180°C. Brush continuously until ribs are golden brown.
6. Pour balance of marinade over ribs and bake for another five minutes. Serves six.

PORK CHOPS WITH PINEAPPLE

4	chops		*	a lump of butter
1	cup pineapple chunks		2	cups shredded cabbage
8	prunes or 1 cup raisins		*	salt
1	teaspoon grated lime peel		¼	cup vinegar
*	sprinkle of sugar and salt		1	tablespoon water
*	breadcrumbs			

1. Brown chops and sprinkle with salt.
2. In a casserole dish, place the chops in layers with the pineapple, prunes, peel and sugar.
3. Cover with breadcrumbs and dot with butter. Bake in a slow oven 300°F for 1½ hours.
4. Serve with shredded cabbage which has been sprinkled with salt and boiled in vinegar and water. When tender, strain and serve hot.

RABBIT FRICASSEE

1	rabbit cut into pieces		2	slices bacon
2	tablespoons vinegar		1	cup chicken broth
*	oil or fat		2	tablespoons raisins
*	salt and pepper		1	dessertspoon grated chocolate
2	sliced onions		1	teaspoon sugar

1. Wash rabbit in vinegar. Pat dry and sauté in fat with sliced onions, bacon and seasonings.
2. Add broth and simmer slowly until rabbit is tender.
3. Add the sugar, chocolate and raisins to finish cooking.
4. Do not be afraid of the chocolate, it gives a surprisingly pleasant flavour to this dish.

ROASTED RABBIT

1	rabbit (skin and clean)		*	salt, pepper
*	sage		1	cup breadcrumbs
1	tablespoon butter		*	bacon drippings
¼	cup milk			

1. Stuff rabbit with bread crumbs mixed with the given ingredients.
2. Sew up cavity.
3. Rub all over with bacon dripping.
4. Roast 1-1½ hrs. in a 350°F oven.

TRIPE WINDSOR

2	lbs. tripe	1	chopped onion
1	qrt. water	4	chopped tomatoes
2	onions	1	tablespoon brandy
2	carrots	2	ozs. margarine
1	cup stock	*	grated nutmeg
*	salt, thyme, parsley to taste	*	salt and pepper

1. Wash tripe with lime juice and put into a stew pot with the water.
2. Simmer for 2 hours. Add vegetables, herbs and salt and simmer until tripe is tender and the vegetables cooked.
3. Remove tripe from the stock and cut into small pieces.
4. Mix tripe and vegetables with remaining ingredients in a covered casserole.
5. Bake in a moderate oven for 35 minutes.

POT ROAST

*	A four-pound cut of beef without bone	2	stalks escallion
1	teaspoon pepper	2	medium onions
3	teaspoons salt		water
	sprig of thyme	2	ozs. Beef salt

1. Combine salt, pepper, thyme, escallion and beef salt.
2. Pierce meat and fill with the mixture of seasoning. Tie to keep in shape. Leave overnight.
3. Heat a large dutch pot. Pour in oil and allow to heat.
4. Put in beef and brown on all sides.
5. Pour in half cup of water at a time and allow to cook slowly over low heat until meet is fully cooked. Allow approximately 2-3 hours of cooking time.
6. When soft, season gravy and add onions and heat until cooked.
7. Cool meat and slice. Serve gravy on slices.

STEWED PEAS

1	pint red peas	2	stalks escallion
½	lb. salted pig's tail		sprig of thyme
½	lb. salted beef	2	cups coconut milk
½	lb. beef stew	1	whole scotch bonnet pepper

1. Soak peas in cold water to soften (preferably overnight).
2. Soak salted meat in cold water to get rid of excess salt (preferably overnight).
3. Place the meat and peas together in a large sauce pan with water. Simmer for about two hours or until tender.
4. Add thyme, escallion, pepper, coconut milk and spinners.
5. Cook for thirty more minutes. Serve hot with white rice.

Vegetables

BEANS IN SOUR CREAM SAUCE

1   lb. green beans (string beans)   *   salt
2   tablespoons butter

    1.   Boil beans uncovered, strain, melt butter, add beans and toss.
    2.   Season with pepper.
    3.   Top with this sauce.

SAUCE
1   cup sour cream   *   a few drops of lime juice,
¼   cup milk   *   a pinch of garlic powder

    Mix ingredients together and pour over beans.

BROAD BEAN CUTLETS

1   lb. broad beans (or sugar beans)   1   teaspoon chopped parsley
1   oz. margarine   6   ozs. crushed potatoes
2   eggs   *   breadcrumbs
1   teaspoon minced onion   *   salt and pepper to taste

    1.   Cook beans in boiling water with salt and onions.
    2.   Puree by rubbing through a sieve.
    3.   Add melted margarine, crushed potatoes, seasoning, and enough of the beaten
         eggs to bind into a paste.
    4.   Add enough bread crumbs to shape into cutlets and coat with more breadcrumbs.
         Fry in deep hot fat.
    5.   Drain and serve warm.

STUFFED BREADFRUIT

1   medium size breadfruit   1   small chopped onion
1   tablespoon butter   *   a pinch of salt
¼   cup milk.

    1.   Stuffed breadfruit is first roasted for an hour in the skin - roasted over charcoal is of
         course the best way, but it can be done over a gas burner.
    2.   When cooked, cut a circle in the top, scoop out heart and discard, then scoop out the flesh.
    3.   Crush this, cream with milk and butter and season with a little salt and onion. To this
         may be added minced beef, codfish and ackee, or left over stew etc.
    4.   Pack into the cavity, wrap with foil and put into the oven to warm through before serving.

BAKED CABBAGE

3	cups shredded cabbage	1	teaspoon salt
2	cups breadcrumbs	1	teaspoon prepared mustard
1	cup grated cheese	2	cups milk
2	eggs	1/8	teaspoon pepper

1. Cover cabbage with water, bring to a boil and drain.
2. In a shallow 2 qrt. dish, arrange cabbage, breadcrumbs and cheese in layers.
3. Beat eggs with salt, pepper and mustard.
4. Add milk and pour over the cabbage.
5. Let stand for 15 minutes. Bake for 45 minutes in a 350°F oven.

FRUITED CABBAGE

½	lbs. shredded cabbage	1	cup water
2	ozs. raisins	1	cup diced pineapple
2	diced onions	*	juice of 1 lime

1. Mix cabbage with fruit and onions.
2. Add 1 cup water, lime juice and a pinch of salt.
3. Cook for about 40 minutes or until liquid has evaporated.

CALLALOO BAKE

1	bunch callaloo cooked and diced	2	tablespoons grated cheese
1	diced onion	¼	cup crushed potatoes
2	slices bacon	1	cup breadcrumbs

1. Mix first three ingredients in a casserole dish.
2. Top with breadcrumbs cheese and potatoes.
3. Bake for about 35 minutes in a moderate oven.

FRUITY CALLALOO

1	bunch callaloo, chopped	*	salt, pepper
1	cup grapefruit juice		

1. Wash and prepare callaloo, add salt and pepper.
2. Put into a pot with grapefruit juice. Cook quickly for 10 minutes.
3. Drain, season to taste and serve.

CARROT AMBROSIA

12	carrots	2	tablespoons sugar
2	tablespoons butter or margarine	2	sliced oranges

1. Glaze 12 small carrots by melting the sugar and butter in a pan and turning the carrots, either sliced or whole, in the mixture over a moderate heat till golden brown.
2. Add 2 sliced oranges and reheat to serve.

MINT GLAZED CARROTS

12	small carrots (pre-cooked)	1	teaspoon mint sauce
¼	cup butter	¼	cup sugar

1. Simmer carrots in, the butter.
2. Add mint sauce and sugar.
3. Cook until sugar has melted.

CAULIFLOWER CUSTARD

1	cauliflower	1	cup milk
2	eggs	*	salt, nutmeg, garlic powder

1. Boil cauliflower in some salt and water. When cool, break off flowerets and put into a greased dish.
2. Beat 2 eggs with milk and garlic powder. Pour over cauliflower. Sprinkle with nutmeg. Bake until set.

CHOCHOS BAKED WITH CHEESE

3	chochos, boiled and sliced	*	dabs of butter or margarine
½	cup grated cheese		

1. Place chocho slices in a casserole dish in alternate layers with grated cheese and dabs of butter ending with cheese.
2. Bake until cheese has melted and is crisp on top.

ACKEE SOUFFLÉ

1	dozen ackees	1	oz. cheese, grated
3	tablespoons butter	*	salt
3	tablespoons flour	*	pepper
1	cup milk	1	teaspoon Worcestershire sauce
4	eggs, separated		

1. Prepare ackees by discarding seeds and taking out pink skin. Wash in salt water. Boil quickly and crush.
2. In a heavy saucepan, melt the butter and stir in flour. Cook for one minute then add the milk gradually, stirring steadily. Continue cooking and stirring until the mixture thickens then add the salt, pepper and Worcestershire sauce. Remove from heat and allow to cool a little.
3. Stir in the grated cheese then beat in the egg yolks one by one. Add the crushed ackee and allow the mixture to cool to room temperature.
4. Preheat the oven to 375°F. Butter a 2½ pint soufflé dish or fireproof casserole dish.
5. Beat the egg whites until stiff. Mix one quarter of the whites into the ackee mixture then fold in the rest. Pour into the prepared dish and bake in the middle of the oven for 30 minutes when the soufflé should be well risen and firm. Serve immediately.

FRIED ACKEES

1	dozen ackees (or more)	*	butter
	salt water		

1. Prepare ackees by discarding seeds and taking out pink skin.
2. Cover in salt water for five minutes. Drain. Fry in hot butter.
3. Drain on paper towels and serve. This recipe can be used for tinned ackees.

BEETS WITH ORANGE SAUCE

6	beets (about 1½ lbs.)	¼	cup orange juice
2	tablespoons sugar	1	tablespoon lime juice
1	tablespoon cornstarch	½	teaspoonful grated orange rind
¼	teaspoon salt	1	tablespoon butter

1. Boil beets in salted water until tender.
2. Drain, reserving the water.
3. Peel the beets and dice.
4. Combine sugar, cornstarch and salt in the top of a double boiler.
5. Gently stir in ¼ cup of the liquid from the cooked beets and the orange juice.
6. Cook over boiling water until thick and smooth stirring constantly.
7. Remove from the heat. Stir in remaining ingredients.
8. Add the diced beets and mix lightly. Keep over hot water until ready to serve.

STUFFED CHOCHO OR SQUASH

3   chochos or 1 small squash
9   tablespoons minced beef
6   tablespoons bread crumbs
1   tablespoon margarine

1   minced onion
*   salt, pepper, oil
*   grated cheese

1.   Cut chochos or squash in half and boil until tender but firm.
2.   Scrape out the inside and dice, being careful not to break the skin.
3.   Sauté onions and minced beef in oil and add diced chocho or squash.
4.   Fill shells, top with bread crumbs and a sprinkle of cheese.
5.   Bake in 350°F oven until brown on top.

CORN FRITTERS

1   tin corn kernels
1   cup milk
1   tablespoon flour

4   tablespoons margarine or butter *
*   pinch of salt

1.   Make a batter of milk, flour and salt.
2.   Fold in whole corn kernels and drop by the spoonful into bubbling butter or margarine.
3.   Fry on both sides.

EGG PLANT (GARDEN EGG) with CHEESE AND TOMATOES

2   large eggplants
2   sliced onions
2   sliced tomatoes
1   cup grated cheese

1½ cups water
2   tablespoons oil
*   salt, pepper and mixed herbs

1.   Peel and slice eggplant. Sprinkle with salt and let stand for 30 minutes. Wash off salt and squeeze dry.
2.   Fry in oil, adding onions and tomatoes. Arrange in layers with cheese in a casserole dish. Add water and seasonings. Bake 45 minutes in a moderate oven.

BAKED SWEET POTATO

*   Allow ½ potato per person
3   baked potatoes in skin
2   tablespoons grated coconut

3   tablespoons Red Stripe Beer
2   ozs. butter
*   salt, cinnamon

1.   Cut potatoes in half, scoop out pulp.
2.   Crush with beer and butter.
3.   Add coconut and salt. Sprinkle with cinnamon and bake through to heat and serve.

OKRA WITH TOMATOES

12	boiled okras	1	oz. flour
4	chopped tomatoes	½	pt. milk
4	tablespoons breadcrumbs	*	salt, pepper, thyme
1	oz. butter		

1. Melt butter, stir in flour for 2 minutes. Remove from heat and add the milk gradually. Season and cook over low heat for 5 minutes.
2. Chop okras, mix with tomatoes and 2 tablespoons of the breadcrumbs. Turn into a baking dish and pour flour-milk mixture over this.
3. Sprinkle with remaining breadcrumbs and bake for about 15 minutes in a moderate oven.

RICE & PEAS

1	cup red peas (soaked overnight)	1	sprig thyme
2	qrts. hot water	1	grated coconut
1	slice salt pork or beef	1	tablespoon oil
3	cups rice	*	a piece of hot pepper
*	salt		

1. Brown onion with salt pork and seasoning.
2. Meanwhile, add 1 cup hot water to grated coconut and squeeze out cream.
3. Place peas in a pot with 2 quarts water and cook until tender.
4. Add salt pork and seasonings and cook for ten minutes.
5. Add rice and cook over low heat until ready. Add hot water if more liquid is needed.

STUFFED PAWPAW (PAPAYA)

1	green pawpaw (just streaked with yellow)	1	sweet pepper
2	onions	1	hot pepper
2	cloves garlic	1	tablespoon breadcrumbs
2	tomatoes	1	egg
2	slices of ham or bacon	*	salt

1. Wash pawpaw. Cut off end and scoop out seeds. Chop onions, garlic, peppers and tomatoes and stew for 20 minutes.
2. Grill bacon and dice. Mix with breadcrumbs, egg and salt. Add to the vegetable stew and pack into pawpaw.
3. Cover with foil and set in a pan with a cup of water to bake in a moderate oven for an hour. Skin should not be eaten.

PUMPKIN PUFF

2	cups hot mashed pumpkin	1	egg beaten
2	tablespoons butter	2	tablespoons flour
2	tablespoons minced onion	*	a tip of baking powder
¼	cup milk	*	salt, pepper

1. Heat oven to 400°F.
2. Combine all ingredients and bake in a casserole dish.
3. Cook for 30 minutes.

YAM CASSEROLE

	Yellow yam boiled and sliced	1	cup white sauce
3	hard boiled eggs	*	salt, pepper
½	cup grated cheese		

1. Place slices of yam alternately with sliced eggs and cheese in a casserole dish. Sprinkle with salt and pepper.
2. Make a white sauce and moisten yam mixture with 1 cup or more. Bake in a moderate oven till cheese is melted.

TURNED CORNMEAL

1	cup cornmeal		thyme
¾	cup water	½	tablespoon oil
¾	cup coconut milk	½	tablespoon black pepper
1	onion chopped finely	½	teaspoon salt
1	tomato diced finely		

1. Pour oil in frying pan and sauté onion, tomato and black pepper.
2. Add water to frying pan and bring to a boil.
3. Mix cornmeal and coconut milk and pour into boiling liquid.
4. Stir repeatedly and add thyme and salt.
5. Cook until mixture is smooth and thick.
6. Saltfish or other meats may be added for an extra twist.

Salads

LOBSTER SALAD

1 cup mayonnaise	1 dessertspoon creole sauce
1 teaspoon onion powder	* shredded lettuce
* lobster meat	* a few drops of lime juice
* dressing	

1. For each person arrange shredded lettuce on a plate.
2. Top with a helping on meat which has been tossed with the dressing.
3. Garnish with olives and strips of celery.

ACKEE SALAD

2 cups boiled ackees	* a few strips of cooked chicken
2 chopped, hard boiled eggs	

1. Prepare ackees and boil for 1 minute.
2. Turn into a colander and run cold water over the ackees, which must be firm.
3. Mix with chopped hard boiled eggs and strips of chicken. Season to taste.

AVOCADO AND GRAPEFRUIT

2 avocados	1 dessertspoon vinegar
2 grapefruits	* salt to taste
1 dessertspoon oil	

1. Peel and remove seeds from avocados.
2. Slice in circles. Place in individual plates.
3. Fill centres with grapefruit segments.
4. Cover with dressing of oil and vinegar.

BROAD BEAN SALAD

½	lb. broad beans (shelled)	1	tablespoon diced sour pickles
1	lb. potatoes	*	salt, pepper, oil and vinegar
2	hard boiled eggs		

1. Boil the beans in some salted water.
2. Boil potatoes.
3. Mix beans, diced potatoes, chopped eggs and pickles and season to taste. Moisten with oil and vinegar.

THREE-BEAN SALAD

1	cup cooked string beans	¼	cup oil
1	cup cooked red beans or peas	½	onion finely chopped
1	cup cooked broad beans	*	chopped mint leaves
½	cup vinegar	*	a pinch of sugar and salt

1. Mix beans together and toss with the last five ingredients.

STRING BEAN SALAD

½	lb. cooked beans	½	chopped onion
1	dessertspoon oil	*	a few peanuts
1	dessertspoon vinegar		

1. Boil beans in salted water.
2. Drain and dry in a cloth.
3. Serve with oil and vinegar dressing and some chopped peanuts and onions.

BREADFRUIT SALAD

1	breadfruit	*	mayonnaise, salt, pepper
2	hardboiled eggs	*	a chopped shallot or small onion

1. Peel, dice, and boil breadfruit till just firm.
2. Combine with eggs, shallot, salt and pepper.
3. Moisten with mayonnaise.

CALLALOO SALAD

1 **lb. callaloo or spinach**	½ **cup mayonnaise**
6 **boiled, sliced potatoes**	* **squeeze of lime juice**
6 **thin slices of cheese**	

1. Plunge callaloo into boiling water for 3 minutes. Drain and chop.
2. Mix with cold sliced potatoes and thin slices of cheese.
3. Dress with mayonnaise to which is added a squeeze of lime juice.

CARROT AND RAISIN SALAD

6 **large carrots**	* **oil and vinegar**
½ **cup raisins**	* **lettuce or cabbage leaves**

1. Shred carrots, mix with raisins and sprinkle with oil and vinegar.
2. Serve on leaves.

CHICKEN SALAD

2 **lbs. chicken**	½ **cup mayonnaise**
2 **cups diced pineapple**	1 **dessertspoon minced parsley**
6 **hard boiled eggs**	* **salt**
1 **cup green peas**	

1. Boil chicken, remove the meat and chill.
2. When chilled mix with pineapple, peas, salt and parsley, and toss with mayonnaise.
3. Finally, crumble in the yolks and garnish with egg whites.

CHOCHO SALAD

3 **chochos peeled sliced and boiled**	* **oil and vinegar**
2 **sliced onions**	* **salt and pepper**

1. Place chochos in a shallow dish.
2. Sprinkle with pepper, salt, oil and vinegar.
3. Cover with sliced onions and some more of the oil and vinegar.

CONCH SALAD

12 young queen conch
3 hot peppers
½ cup vinegar
¼ cup oil

2 sliced onions
* salt
* lime juice

1. Cover conch with water and bring to a boil, by which time it should be easy to remove the meat. Wash with lime juice and clean.
2. Dice and mix with chopped hot peppers, vinegar, oil, sliced onions and salt. This is a popular salad in the Bahamas.

CUCUMBER AND SOUR CREAM SALAD

1 cup sour cream
1 teaspoon vinegar
1 tablespoon chopped mint

* a pinch of sugar
* sliced cucumbers

1. Mix together sour cream, vinegar, mint and sugar.
2. Pour this over the sliced cucumbers.
3. Marinate for an hour before serving.

JAMAICAN SALAD

1 cup freshly grated coconut
2 cups finely shredded cabbage
1 cup pineapple cubes

1 cup mayonnaise
* lettuce leaves

1. Combine coconut, cabbage and pineapple with mayonnaise mixing well.
2. Chill and serve on lettuce leaves.

ONION SALAD

12 small onions
2 chopped tomatoes
* a handful of currants or raisins

* salt - parsley
* oil and vinegar to taste

1. Peel and boil onions in a small amount of salted water.
2. When cooked add tomatoes, oil, vinegar, parsley and currants. Serve cold.

SWEET PEPPER SALAD

2	red sweet peppers	2	tablespoons oil
2	green sweet peppers	*	oil and vinegar to taste

1. Cut and slice peppers.
2. Take out veins and seeds.
3. Sauté quickly in oil.
4. Drain. Add oil and vinegar with a pinch of salt.

POTATO SALAD

6	boiled diced potatoes	1	tablespoon chopped parsley
½	diced onion	6	boiled and sliced frankfurters
1	tablespoon flour		(or vienna sausage)
1	tablespoon vinegar	2	tablespoons oil
1	teaspoon sugar	*	salt, pepper

1. Fry frankfurters, with onion in some oil.
2. Add 1 tablespoon flour and blend.
3. Add sugar, vinegar, parsley, salt and pepper.
4. Mix together well and pour over the potatoes. Toss lightly.

PUMPKIN SALAD

½	pumpkin, peeled and boiled	1	dessertspoon vinegar
1	teaspoon mixed herbs	*	a few lettuce leaves
1	tablespoon oil		

1. Place slices of firm boiled pumpkin on lettuce leaves.
2. Make a dressing of herbs and oil and pour over pumpkin.

RICE OR MACARONI SALAD

2	cups cold cooked rice or macaroni	*	herbs
2	ozs. lean ham	2	red sweet peppers
4	stalks escallion	2	green sweet peppers
1	tomato	2	tablespoons oil
4	slices cucumber	*	oil and vinegar to taste

1. Mix diced vegetables and rice with herbs and ham.
2. Pour dressing over salad.

DRESSING

1	dessertspoon oil	1	teaspoon soya sauce
1	dessertspoon vinegar		

Mix well together.

SHRIMP SALAD WITH COCONUT CREAM

1	cup milk	2	chopped sweet peppers
1	cup grated coconut	2	tablespoons soya sauce
1	tablespoon oil	1	tablespoon chopped peanuts
1	teaspoon salt	2	lbs. shrimp (cooked and peeled)
2	minced shallots		

1. Combine milk and coconut in saucepan and bring to boil. Remove from heat and soak for 30 minutes.
2. Press through a sieve to extract cream. Discard pulp.
3. Heat oil, and fry the shallots and peppers.
4. Remove from heat. Add soya sauce and peanuts. Combine with coconut cream.
5. Arrange shrimp on a dish and pour dressing over them. Reserve a few shrimp for garnish and chill slightly to serve.

SALAD CREOLE

$2/3$	pineapple	*	pinch of salt
$1/3$	of a tomato per person	*	squeeze of lime juice
½	cup fresh cream	*	chopped onion
1	tablespoon ketchup		

1. Cut pineapple into thin strips and dice tomato.
2. Combine next 4 ingredients and pour over salad.
3. Serve on lettuce leaves and top with a sprinkle of chopped onions.

TROPICAL SALAD

1	cup grated coconut	1	cup seeded tangerine segments
1	cup diced pineapple	1	cup mayonnaise

1. Combine ingredients and serve on cabbage leaves or lettuce leaves.

Dressing & Sauces

COOKED SALAD DRESSING

2 ozs. butter
1 beaten egg
½ cup milk
¼ cup sugar

1 teaspoon dry mustard
½ cup vinegar
* pinch of salt

1.   Melt butter. Add egg and milk and stir in sugar, salt and mustard, which have been blended with some vinegar.
2.   Gradually add the rest of vinegar. Stir over low heat in a double boiler until thickened. Do not allow to boil.
3.   Cool and refrigerate.

HONEY DRESSING FOR FRUIT SALADS

½ cup vinegar
2 tablespoons honey

½ cup lime juice
3 tablespoons crushed pineapple

1.   Mix together and chill.

A BASIC WHITE SAUCE

1 tablespoon margarine
½ cup flour

1 cup milk
* salt

1.   Melt 2 tablespoons margarine on low heat.
2.   Add ½ cup flour slowly, whilst stirring with 1 cup of milk, and a pinch of salt until this thickens.
3.   Do not allow to burn.

A HOT DRESSING

½ cup peanut butter
¼ cup tomato ketchup

¼ cup milk
* a few-drops hot sauce

1.   Mix to a paste adding more milk if needed.
2.   Use over onions, cucumbers or sweet peppers.

OIL AND VINEGAR

¼	cup oil	1	dry mustard
¹⁄₆	cup vinegar	*	pinch of salt

Mix well together.

MY SALAD DRESSING

¼	cup vinegar	1	teaspoon mint jelly
2	teaspoons sugar	*	a squeeze of lime and a pinch of salt

Blend together and chill.

A DRESSING FOR SEA FOOD

4	tablespoons mayonnaise	1	teaspoon lime juice
4	tablespoons french dressing	*	a pinch of curry powder
2	tablespoons mango chutney	*	salt and pepper to taste

Combine and mix all ingredients.

SPICY DRESSING

3	tablespoons vinegar	1	tablespoon powdered ginger
2	tablespoons sugar		

Blend together and chill. Delicious on crisp green salad.

TWO MINUTE MAYONNAISE

1	teaspoon sugar	½	cup evaporated milk
½	teaspoon salt	½	cup oil
¼	teaspoon dry mustard	2	tablespoons vinegar

1. Mix all ingredients except oil and vinegar.
2. Add oil gradually in a thin stream and beat well.
3. Finally, add vinegar slowly, continuing to beat till smooth.

DEVIL'S SAUCE

2 tablespoons brown sugar	1 tablespoon guava jelly
1 dessertspoon creole sauce	¼ teaspoon salt
3 tablespoons ketchup	3 tablespoons vinegar
¼ teaspoon hot sauce	

1. Mix all ingredients together in a saucepan and simmer for 2 minutes.
2. Cool and chill.

EGG SAUCE

½ pt. evaporated milk	1 teaspoon lime juice
2 eggs	½ teaspoon pepper and salt
1 teaspoon vinegar	

1. Hard boil eggs and chop.
2. Mix with milk and other ingredients. Excellent over salads.

HOT PEPPER SAUCE

4 hot peppers	1 teaspoon ketchup
1 teaspoon oil	1 teaspoon vinegar
1 teaspoon creole sauce	* salt to taste

1. Put peppers, and other ingredients through a blender or mincer.
2. Bottle. Makes 1 bottle.

MARINA SAUCE

¼ cup oil	3 cups diced tomatoes
1 clove crushed garlic	1 chopped sweet pepper
2 teaspoons minced parsley	* salt to taste

Mix well together and simmer slowly for 30 minutes. Cool and chill.

MARMALADE SAUCE

6 teaspoons dry mustard	2 teaspoons rum
* marmalade to taste	* soya sauce

1. Mix mustard with some rum to make a paste.
2. Add marmalade and a few drops of soya sauce.
3. Serve with barbecued dishes.

PEANUT SAUCE

2 cups crushed peanuts	3 cups water
1 tablespoon chopped onion	2 teaspoons curry powder
3 tomatoes	* salt
1 tablespoon fat	

1. Put nuts into salted water and boil for 15 minutes.
2. Fry onions and tomatoes and add to peanut mixture with curry powder.
3. Simmer for about 20 minutes, stirring frequently.

PEPPERMINT SAUCE

2 egg whites	1 tablespoon sugar
2 cups thin cream (evaporated milk)	2 tablespoons crème de menthe

1. Beat egg whites stiff.
2. Fold in cream, sugar and crème de menthe.
3. Good over a fruit salad.

RUM SAUCE

4 ozs. butter	2 tablespoons rum
2 ozs. granulated sugar	

1. Cream butter and sugar and add rum very slowly.
2. Beat well and keep cool.

SABAYON SAUCE

4 ozs. sugar	3 egg yolks
2 tablespoons sherry	* few drops vanilla

1. Cream sugar and yolks together over a gentle heat.
2. Add vanilla. Gradually add sherry and whisk vigorously until frothy and firm.
3. Use immediately.

SWEET AND SOUR SAUCE

6 chopped shallots	1½ cups pineapple juice
2 tablespoons vinegar	1 teaspoon soya sauce
1½ tablespoons brown sugar	½ cup water
½ teaspoon ketchup	3 teaspoons cornstarch

1. Mix all ingredients except water and cornstarch and simmer gently for about 40 minutes.
2. Mix cornstarch with water and add to the sauce.
3. Simmer 5 minutes more, stirring until sauce thickens.

Jamaican Jerk

TASTY JERK PORK BITES

1	lb. jerk pork	½	teaspoon powdered ginger
1	small onion	2	teaspoons Pickapeppa sauce
1	small country pepper	2	ozs. rum

1. Cut jerk pork into small pieces and place in blender.
2. Remove seeds from country pepper and place in blender with other ingredients.
3. Blend until smooth. Chill.
4. Serve on small, bite-size crackers.

JERK SAUSAGE IN BACON BLANKET

6 Jerk Sausages*   ½ lb. bacon

1. Cut sausages into 3-4 pieces.
2. Wrap sausage pieces in bacon and fasten with toothpick.
3. Bake or grill for approximately 10 minutes just before serving. Serve hot. Yields 18-24.

May be purchased pre-prepared

THE AUTHENTIC JAMAICAN JERK SAUCE

½	lb. Scotch Bonnet Peppers*	2	tbls. whole pimento (allspice) berries
1	small onion, chopped	1½	tbls. ground ginger
3	stalks scallion, chopped	1	tsp. nutmeg, freshly grated
3	sprigs fresh thyme, chopped	½	cup white vinegar
3	tbls. Salt	¼	cup soy sauce
2	tbls. black pepper		

In a food processor or blender, puree all ingredients until the sauce is coarse, yet pourable. Makes about 2-3 cups.

May be adjusted as desired.

49

JERKED PORK SNACKS

1 3-4 lbs. deboned leg of pork (cut into bite size pieces)	* chopped onion and garlic
1 cup vinegar	* crushed pimento leaves
* chopped hot pepper	* pimento grains, salt

1. Marinate the pieces of pork in the marinade for 4 days turning frequently. Keep covered in refrigerator.
2. Take out and wipe dry. Cook pork on a grid over burning coals to get a smokey flavour; however, it can also be baked crisp on a baking sheet in the oven.

JERK PORK

4	lbs. boneless pork shoulder roast	2	tbsp. onion powder
3	tbsp. salt	½	tsp. ground allspice
1	tbsp. black pepper	1	tbsp. soy sauce
3	tbsp. garlic powder	½	cup jerk sauce

1. Cut pork shoulder into two pieces.
2. Using a butcher knife, make cuts 1" apart and 1/8 to ¼" deep.
3. This will help the marinade soak into the roast.
4. Place in a shallow pan.
5. In a bowl, combine remaining ingredients.
6. Rub sauce over pork.
7. Cover and refrigerator overnight.
8. Preheat barbecue to 300°F.
9. Slow cook pork until meat is brown and tender, about 45 minutes to 1 hour or until meat thermometer inserted into meat reaches 160°F.
10. To serve, cut pork into 1" cubes.

JERK CHICKEN

1	3 lb. chicken, clean and quartered	½	tsp. paprika
1	tsp. salt	4	tbsp. jerk sauce
½	tsp. black pepper		

1. Using a small knife, make two slits in each chicken quarter.
2. Season with salt, pepper, paprika, and jerk sauce. Cover and marinate in the refrigerator for at least 1 hour or even overnight.
3. Preheat oven to 375°F and barbecue to 350°F.
4. Place chicken in a roasting pan and cook in the oven for 30 minutes. Then transfer chicken to the barbecue and grill, turning chicken often, until it is cooked through.

JERKED AND BUTTERFLIED JUMBO SHRIMP

15	jumbo or Black tiger shrimp, butterflied	½	tsp. cayenne pepper
3	tbsp. olive oil	3	lemon wedges
1	tbsp. jerk sauce		

1. Preheat oven to 400°F.bgy
2. Arrange shrimp on a greased baking sheet.
3. In a small bowl, combine olive oil, jerk sauce, and the juice from one of the wedges of lemon.
4. Brush shrimp with mixture then sprinkle lightly with cayenne pepper.
5. Broil for 7 to 10 minutes. Serve hot, garnished with remaining lemon wedges. Serves 4 to 6.

JERK SNAPPER STUFFED WITH CALLALOO

3	1-lb. whole red snappers, scaled and cleaned	2	tsp. olive oil
1	tbsp. lime juice	1	small onion, sliced
3	cups water	1	medium carrot, cut into strips
1	tsp. salt	6	whole okra, cut in half, lengthwise
1	tsp. black pepper	1	cup canned callaloo or 1½ cups of fresh spinach, chopped 4 tbsp. butter
4	tbsp. jerk sauce		fresh lime wedges (garnish)

1. Preheat oven to 375°F, or barbecue to 350°F.
2. In a large bowl, wash fish with water and lime juice.
3. Season with salt, pepper and 1 tbsp. of the jerk sauce. Set aside.
4. In a separate bowl, combine remaining jerk sauce, olive oil, onion, carrot, okra and callaloo or spinach.
5. Stuff mixture into fish cavity. Dot each fish with 1 tbsp. butter. Lightly grease foil with olive oil or non-stick spray.
6. Wrap each fish in foil. Bake in the oven or on the barbecue for 20 to 30 minutes. Serves 2 to 4.

JERK PRAWNS

12	large Black tiger shrimp	1	tsp. vegetable oil
½	tsp. salt	1	tsp. jerk sauce
½	tsp. black pepper		lime wedges (garnish)

1. In a medium bowl, season shrimp with salt and pepper.
2. In a separate bowl, combine oil and jerk sauce. Pour over prawns.
3. Preheat barbecue or grill to 375°F.
4. Grill shrimp 7 minutes each side or until they are bright pink.
5. Serve garnished with lime wedges. Serves 2.

JERK MEATBALLS

1	lb. ground beef	1	tbsp. garlic powder
1	small onion, finely chopped	1	egg
½	cup breadcrumbs	1	stalk escallion, finely chopped
2	tbsp. jerk sauce	1	tbsp. soy sauce

1. Preheat oven to 350°F.
2. In a large bowl, combine all ingredients.
3. Roll into 2" round balls.
4. Bake on a greased baking sheet for 20 minutes. Serves 4 to 6.

JERK LAMB CHOPS

8	lamb chops, ½ inch thick	1	sprig fresh thyme, chopped
1	tsp. jerk sauce	3	tbsp. olive oil
1	clove garlic, chopped		salt and black pepper to taste

1. In a large baking dish, season chops with all ingredients.
2. Cover and marinate in the refrigerator for 1 hour.
3. Preheat oven to 400°F or barbecue to 375°F.
4. On a greased baking pan, bake chops for 10 minutes.
5. Turn on broiler and broil chops 3 to 5 minutes each side.
6. On a barbecue, grill chops 10 minutes each side. Serves 6.

JERK WINGS

1	tbsp. vegetable oil	1	tbsp. barbecue sauce
2	tbsp. jerk sauce	2	lbs. chicken wings, tips removed

1. In a large bowl, combine oil, jerk sauce, and barbecue sauce.
2. Add wings, cover, and marinate in the refrigerator for at least 20 minutes.
3. Preheat barbecue to 375°F.
4. Grill wings for 30-40 minutes, or until well done. Serves 4 to 6.

COCONUT GIZZADAS

STUFFED ROAST PORK

GUAVA MOUSSE

LOBSTER CREOLE

PEANUT CAKE

OXTAIL AND BEANS

Barbecues

BARBECUE COOKING CHART

RARE	4 - 5 lbs.	Roast 2 - 2½ hrs.
MEDIUM	4 - 5 lbs.	Roast 2½ - 3 hrs.
WELL DONE	4 - 5 lbs.	Roast 3 - 4 hrs.

BEEF LIVER IN BARBECUE SAUCE

1	lb. beef liver cut in ¼" slices	1	tablespoon Pickapeppa sauce
2	tablespoons butter or margarine	1	teaspoon sugar
1	cup sliced onions	1	teaspoon prepared mustard
½	cup green sweet pepper, cut up	¼	cup tomato ketchup
1	tablespoon vinegar	½	teaspoon hot pepper sauce
*	salt and black pepper		

1. Start heating oven to 325°F. Cut liver slices in half crosswise. Place half of slices side by side, in covered, shallow baking dish; sprinkle lightly with salt and pepper.
2. Sauté onion and sweet pepper in butter or margarine and arrange half on liver. Mix vinegar with next five ingredients with rest of liver then rest of sauce.
3. Bake uncovered for 10 minutes. Makes 4 servings. The family will need no encouragement to try this dish.

BACON-WRAPPED FRANKFURTERS

8	rashers bacon	1	lb. frankfurters
4	teaspoons mustard	4	ozs. cheddar cheese, sliced

1. Barbecue the frankfurters over medium coals for about 15 minutes, then slice them lengthways, almost through. Fill with cheese slices and press the frankfurters together again.
2. Spread the rashers of bacon with mustard and wrap around the frankfurters, securing the ends with wooden cocktail sticks.
3. Place on the grill again and cook over medium coals for a further 5 minutes, or until cheese melts and bacon is crisp.
4. Serve with a mixed green salad and potato chips. Serves 4.

BAKED RED SNAPPER IN SAVOURY BARBECUE SAUCE

1	3 lb. red snapper		Pickapeppa sauce
6	tablespoons butter	1	tablespoon ketchup
½	cup chopped onions	1	teaspoon chili powder
2	cups chopped celery	½	lemon, finely sliced
¼	cup chopped green peppers	1	teaspoon salt
3	cups canned tomatoes	2	bay leaves
1	tablespoon Worcestershire /	2	teaspoons sugar
	Pickapeppa sauce	1	red pepper

1. Preheat oven to 350°F. Dredge snapper inside and out with seasoned flour baking pan.
2. In a pot, melt butter. Add onions, celery and green peppers.
3. Simmer until celery is tender. Add other remaining ingredients and simmer 15 minutes.
4. Pour sauce over the fish. Bake approximately 45 minutes, basting frequently. Serves 4 - 5 people.

BARBECUED CHICKEN

1	2 ½ lb. chicken, cut in serving pieces	*	salt to taste
*	black pepper	*	garlic

SAUCE

¼	cup chopped onions	¼	teaspoon paprika
½	cup water	½	teaspoon salt
2	tablespoons vinegar	1	teaspoon black pepper
1	tablespoon Worcestershire/	1	teaspoon prepared mustard
	Pickapeppa sauce	1	teaspoon ketchup
¼	cup lemon juice	1	tablespoon butter
2	tablespoons sugar	*	hot pepper sauce to taste
1	cup chili/tomato sauce		

1. Season chicken liberally with salt, black pepper, garlic. Let stand 1 hour.
2. To prepare sauce: Sauté onions till brown. Add other sauce ingredients and simmer
3. 15 minutes, then cool.
4. Broil chicken. Add sauce when chicken is nearly done (after about 1 hour), basting continually. Serves 4.

BARBECUED CHICKEN WITH SPECIAL SAUCE

1	3 lb. chicken	1	teaspoon dry mustard
1	cup tomato sauce or ketchup	1	teaspoon sugar
1	teaspoon creole sauce	*	a drop or two of hot sauce
2	tablespoons vinegar		

1. Cut chicken into pieces.
2. Season with salt and pepper and grill over hot coals basting frequently with sauce made by combining last 6 ingredients and bring to a boil.

BARBECUED CHICKEN WINGS

2   lbs. chicken wings
3   tablespoons honey
3   tablespoons vinegar
2   tablespoons sugar
3   tablespoons soy sauce

1   large clove garlic, crushed
1   stock cube
¼   pint hot water
1   tablespoon sherry

1.   Cut and trim chicken wings. Place in a bowl.
2.   Blend together honey, vinegar, sugar, soy sauce and garlic, and pour over the meat.
3.   Dissolve stock cube in the hot water, then add the sherry. Add to the other ingredients in the bowl and stir together.
4.   Leave to marinate for 8 to 12 hours or overnight in the refrigerator. Preheat the oven to moderately slow at 335°F.
5.   Arrange chicken wings on a rack in a roast pan and baste well with the marinade.
6.   Bake, uncovered, until golden brown, basting occasionally with the sauce, turning once during the cooking time. If served as a party-time snack, eat with fingers and provide a finger bowl of warm water and serviettes to wipe fingers.

BARBECUED LAMB CHOPS

4   lbs. lamb chops
1   teaspoon prepared mustard
1   piece ginger, beaten
2   medium-sized onions, sliced
1   tablespoon salad oil
1   cup water
*   salt to taste

2   tablespoons chili/tomato sauce
1   tablespoon Worcestershire/
    Pickapeppa sauce
1   tablespoon vinegar
*   hot pepper sauce to taste
*   black pepper

1.   Season chops with mustard, ginger, salt and pepper. Place sliced onions over chops in baking pan.
2.   Combine other ingredients and pour over onions and chops. Bake, covered, in moderate oven, basting frequently, for approximately 15-20 minutes or until done. Remove lid 10 minutes before chops are cooked. Serves 6.

BARBECUED ORIENTAL CHICKEN

1   cup soy sauce
1   cup sake (Japanese rice wine) or
    1 cup grapefruit juice or 1 cup dry sherry
¼   cup cooking oil

1   teaspoon sugar
½   teaspoon grated fresh ginger root or
    ground ginger
*   one 2½ pound chicken, cut up

1.   Mix together soy sauce, sake or grapefruit juice or sherry, sugar and ginger in a large shallow dish. Add chicken, turning to coat both sides.
2.   Cover and marinate in refrigerator, several hours or overnight, turning occasionally. Remove chicken from marinade and brush with oil.
3.   Grill about 6 inches from source of heat, brushing with marinade and turning frequently until brown and tender. Serves 4.

BARBECUED MEAT BALLS

1 lb. ground beef	1 egg yolk
2 tablespoons chopped parsley	1 tablespoon soft butter
1 tablespoon bread crumbs	1 teaspoon lemon juice
1 teaspoon salt	1 teaspoon black pepper
½ large onion	1 small sweet pepper
1 sprig thyme, chopped	2 whole pimento grains

SAUCE

1 large sweet pepper	1 large onion
1 clove garlic	1 carrot (cut up in long strips)
1 cup ketchup	2 tablespoons sugar
1 teaspoon vinegar	½ teaspoon salt (to taste)
1 piece ginger	

1. To prepare sauce: sauté sweet pepper, onion, garlic, carrot in butter.
2. Add other ingredients, then simmer for 20 minutes.
3. Meanwhile, combine meatball ingredients, mold into balls.
4. Skewer balls and place over flame, turning and basting continually with sauce. Serves 4.

BARBECUED PERCH

5 lbs. perch	1 tablespoon Worcestershire/
1 cup celery	Pickapeppa sauce
1 cup onions	2 tablespoons vinegar
1 cup ketchup	2 tablespoons sugar
1 tablespoon prepared mustard	

1. Grill fish for 10 minutes. Meanwhile, sauté celery and onions.
2. Combine other ingredients, bring to a boil. Baste fish with sauce, cooking for another 10 minutes. Serves 6-8.

BARBECUED SPARERIBS (BAKED)

Use the American style pork spareribs for this succulent recipe. If you can do the ribs over a good bed of charcoal, attending carefully to the basting, so much the better!

5-6 lbs. spareribs cut in serving pieces	2 tablespoons lemon juice
1 lemon thinly sliced	1' teaspoon chili powder
¼ cup molasses	1 tablespoon celery seed
¼ cup prepared mustard	2 tablespoons Pickapeppa sauce
2 tablespoons vinegar	½ cup tomato ketchup
* salt to taste	

1. Place spareribs, meat side up, in a shallow pan. Sprinkle with salt. Top with lemon slices. Bake in a moderate oven 350°F for 30 minutes.
2. Combine remaining ingredients and blend well. Remove lemon slices. Brush spareribs with mixture; turn and continue baking one hour longer, basting frequently. Serve hot.

BARBECUED SPARE RIBS

2	lbs. spare ribs, cut in serving pieces	¼	oz. garlic powder
2	teaspoons salt	¼	oz. onion powder
4	pimento grains, crushed	½	cup paprika
*	oregano	¼	cup lemon juice

SAUCE

¼	cup chopped onions	2	tablespoons brown sugar
1	tablespoon fat	½	cup chili/tomato sauce
½	cup water	½	teaspoon paprika
2	tablespoons vinegar	1	teaspoon black pepper
1	tablespoon Worcestershire/ Pickapeppa sauce	1	teaspoon prepared mustard
		*	hot pepper sauce to taste

1. Season ribs with mixture of salt, oregano, garlic, onion and paprika. Rub into meat well.
2. Place ribs in moderate oven with a small amount of water, and cover. Cook for approximately ½ hour until almost tender. Remove from oven and cool.
3. Place ribs on rack over coals, and turn continually until done (approximately 10 minutes).
4. Make sauce by combining all ingredients and simmering for 10 minutes. Just a few minutes removing from rack, brush ribs with sauce.

BARBECUED STANDING RIBS (BEEF)

8-10 lbs. ribs		*	black pepper
*	salt	*	garlic powder

SAUCE

14	ozs. ketchup	1	teaspoon coriander
½	cup white vinegar	⅛	teaspoon paprika
1	teaspoon sugar	⅛	teaspoon saffron
⅛	teaspoon salt	¼	teaspoon ground ginger
½	teaspoon cumin	1	red pepper, finely chopped

1. Season ribs liberally with salt, pepper, garlic powder; let stand overnight. When ready to cook, skewer beef, and cook over coals, turning very slowly, for about 2-3 hours.
2. Meanwhile, combine sauce ingredients, simmer 15 minutes. Baste ribs with sauce only 15 minutes before removing from coals.
3. Serves 15 people.
4. To add an extra special touch, orange juice can be added to the basting mixture.

BARBECUED STEAK

2-2½	lbs. sirloin steak	1	cup tomato sauce
8	ozs. olive oil	2	tablespoons brown sugar
¼	cup soy sauce	1	green pepper, cut in chunks
*	salt to taste	1	onion, sliced
*	black pepper		

1. Season steak with salt and pepper. Combine other ingredients, pour over steak.
2. Marinate in refrigerator 4 hours or overnight, turning occasionally. Broil steak. Serves 4.

CHRISTMAS HAM WITH BARBECUE SAUCE

1	12-15 lb. Ham	2	tablespoons mustard
1	cup brown sugar	1	cup sherry

1. Preheat oven to 325°F. Bake ham, allowing 25 minutes per pound. When ham is almost done, remove from oven, score and add cloves.
2. Make a mixture of brown sugar and mustard, then add sherry.
3. Mixture should be like a thick paste. Coat thickly over ham, then bake for another ½ hour.

JIFFY BARBECUE SAUCE

½	cup tomato ketchup	2	teaspoons Pickapeppa Sauce
1	teaspoon dry mustard	*	liquid from the can of corn & water
1	teaspoon hot pepper sauce		to make ¾ cup
2	teaspoons mango chutney		

Combine all ingredients and pour over pork chops.

MEAT LOAF WITH BARBECUE SAUCE

LOAF
1½	lbs. ground beef	3	strips bacon, cut in small pieces
½	lb. ground lean pork	½	cup bread crumbs

GARNISH
8	bacon strips

SAUCE
2	tablespoons ketchup	2	tablespoons salt
¼	teaspoon Worchestershire/ Pickapeppa sauce	*	parsley sprigs
½	cup tomato juice	¼	teaspoon chili powder
2	eggs	1	tablespoon minced onion
2	tablespoons minced onions	2	tablespoons vinegar

1. Combine all loaf ingredients. Shape into individual loaves (makes 8 loaves).
2. Wrap a strip of bacon around each loaf.
3. Simmer sauce ingredients for 15 minutes, then pour over loaves. Bake at 350°F for 45 minutes, basting once or twice during baking.

ORANGE GRILLED FISH

2   lbs. firm white fish

MARINADE

4   tablespoons soy sauce
2   tablespoons tomato ketchup
2   tablespoons chopped parsley

½   cup orange juice
*   grated rind of ½ orange
*   salt and black pepper

1.   Cut the fish into 1" pieces. Mix the ingredients for the marinade together, beating well. Pour over the fish and leave to marinate for 1 hour.
2.   Drain the fish and thread on six skewers. Grill over hot coals for about 8 minutes, then turn and grill for a further 7 minutes.
3.   Baste with the marinade during cooking. Serves 6.

SHRIMP WITH COLD BARBECUE SAUCE

2   lbs. fresh shrimp
½   cup finely chopped celery
1   stalk scallion
6   tablespoons olive oil
3   tablespoons lemon juice
¼   cup ketchup
1   clove garlic

¼   teaspoon hot pepper sauce
5   tablespoons horseradish
2   tablespoons prepared mustard
¼   teaspoon paprika
¾   teaspoon salt
½   teaspoon white pepper

1.   Clean then poach shrimp.
2.   To prepare sauce: rub bowl with garlic, then combine other ingredients.
3.   Marinate shrimp in sauce for an hour. Serve chilled on a bed of lettuce.

SMOKED PORK CHOPS, BAKED WITH JIFFY BARBECUE SAUCE

6   smoked pork chops
1   can whole kernel corn
1   egg, well beaten
1   cup chopped celery

1   onion, chopped
2   tablespoons oil
1   ounce margarine
1   green sweet pepper, chopped

1.   Sauté celery, onion and sweet green pepper in margarine, and mix with corn & egg.
2.   Brown chops lightly in oil, drain and arrange in a casserole dish.
3.   Cover with the corn mixture and pour sauce all over.
4.   Bake covered at 350°F for one hour. Remove cover during last 10 minutes.

SPICY ROAST BEEF BARBECUE

1	(4 - 5) Beef rump roast, rolled and tied	½	teaspoon Pimento
½	cup butter	½	teaspoon coriander
1	cup vinegar	¼	teaspoon chili powder
½	teaspoon dry mustard	1	tablespoon lemon juice
1	tablespoon minced onion	⅓	cup brown sugar
1	tablespoon Pickapeppa Sauce	*	salt and pepper to taste

1. Leave roast at room temperature for at least on hour.
2. Start the fire in the barbecue, and let the charcoal bed burn until charcoal turns ash gray in colour.
3. Tap the gray ash from the coals with fire tongs. After you start the fire, skewer the roast on the spit rod, through the centre of the roast (if it is not centred properly, the spit will not turn.) Insert holding forks.
4. When the fire is ready, start to brown the roast. While the roast is browning, combine the sauce ingredients in a saucepan, and heat until the butter melts. Makes about 2 cups. When roast is an even brown on all sides start to baste with the sauce, basting every 20 minutes until done.

(See Cooking Chart)

Pickles & Preserves

BREAD AND BUTTER PICKLES

1 qrt. sliced cucumbers	1 sliced green pepper
2 sliced onions	1 chopped clove garlic

1. Place onions, cucumbers, pepper, garlic and salt in a pan. Cover with ice cubes and let stand for 2 hours. Drain.
2. Combine other ingredients and pour over onion mixture. Heat to boil for a few minutes only. Seal while still hot in jars. Makes approximately 4 jars.

CORN RELISH

12 young corn ears	2 teaspoons flour
3 peppers (remove seeds)	4 cups vinegar
1½ cups sugar	4 onions
2 tablespoons salt	* mustard to taste

1. Remove corn from the cob. Put onions and pepper through a mincer and mix with corn. Cover with 3 cups of vinegar.
2. To remaining cup of vinegar add sugar, salt, flour and mustard to make a paste. Add this to vegetable mixture and bring to a slow boil for 30 minutes.
3. Pour into hot jars and seal.

HOT PEPPERS AND SHALLOTS

6 hot peppers	1 clove
2 cups white vinegar	* salt
* shallots to fill 2 jars	* pimento grains

1. Slice peppers and remove seeds.
2. Peel and wash shallots.
3. Fill jars with shallots and hot pepper slices. Boil vinegar with spices and salt.
4. Pour over peppers and shallots and seal.

MANGO CHUTNEY

2	ozs. green ginger	1	oz. garlic powder
2	lbs. brown sugar	2	ozs. salt
1	lb. green mangoes - peeled and sliced	1	sliced hot pepper
1	lb. raisins	1	sliced onion
1	tablespoon soya sauce		

1. Crush the ginger. Mix all ingredients and bring to a boil.
2. Simmer gently until chutney is thick and syrupy.
3. Correct seasoning.

RED DEVIL

6	peppers, seeded and diced	1	teaspoon nutmeg
3	diced onions	*	pinch of salt
1	pint vinegar		

1. Put hot peppers and onions through a mincer.
2. Combine with vinegar, nutmeg and salt and bring to a boil.
3. Bottle when cool.

TO PRESERVE FRESH TOMATOES

1. Choose firm, ripe, small tomatoes without blemish.
2. Put them into a jar with a large mouth.
3. Fill jar with oil (corn oil preferably) so that tomatoes are covered with a layer of oil 1' deep. On top of oil pour a little brandy or rum and seal.

PICKLED WATERMELON

2	lbs. sugar	4	cloves
2	quarts water	1	piece hot pepper
¼	cup salt	*	pieces of cinnamon stick (or grated nutmeg)
1	pint vinegar		
*	peel of watermelon		

1. Peel off outer green skin of watermelon and chop the white flesh into pieces. Cover with water and salt and simmer until tender.
2. Bring remaining ingredients to a boil for 10 minutes. Add tender melon to this and continue to simmer until melon is transparent. Pack in jars. Approx. 4 jars.

VEGETABLE RELISH

6	carrots	1	cucumber
1	pepper, seeds removed	6	olives
2	onions	2	cups water
2	chochos		

1. Chop carrots, peppers, onions, chochos, cucumbers and olives, add water to cover. Bring to a boil to tenderize.
2. Drain.

DRESSING

½	cup oil	1	tablespoon hot pepper sauce
1	cup vinegar	*	salt to taste
2	tablespoons ketchup		

1. Mix dressing and bring to a boil.
2. Pour dressing over the vegetables, which have been packed in sterilized jars.
3. Makes 4 jars.

GARLIC VINEGAR

Steep garlic cloves, which have been pricked with a pin, in vinegar for 10 days. Use for salad dressings.

HERB VINEGARS

Various herb vinegars can be made by loosely packing a jar with a combination of herbs and filling with vinegar. Stand jar in a saucepan of water and bring to a boil slowly. Then allow to cool. After two weeks vinegar will be ready for use.

PEPPER WINE

Fill ¾ bottle with either cherry or bird peppers. Fill up with sherry or rum. Allow to stand for about one week before using.

Jellies & Jams

PINEAPPLE JAM

1   pineapple
*   sugar

*   nutmeg
     Peel and grate the pineapple.

1.   To each lb. of pineapple pulp, add ¾ lb. of sugar.
2.   Add nutmeg to taste. Boil and stir until mixture thickens and sugar is melted.
3.   Seal in jars whilst hot. Makes approx. 3 jars.

PUMPKIN JAM

3   lbs. pumpkin
2   lbs. sugar
1   lime

1   orange
*   salt

1.   Peel and cut pumpkin into slices, then dice and pack in a jar. Add sugar. Cover and stand for 12 hours.
2.   Drain off liquid and boil until syrupy. Add pumpkin, sliced lime and orange.
3.   Stir in a pinch of salt. Boil up, and cook until clear.
4.   Seal in jars. Makes approx. 6 jars.

TOMATO JAM

8   tomatoes peeled and chopped
2   tablespoons lime juice
4   cups sugar

2   tablespoons chopped raisins
½   teaspoon all spice

1.   Simmer tomatoes for 10 minutes.
2.   Add all ingredients except sugar and bring to a boil.
3.   Add sugar and continue to boil until sugar melts and mixture thickens. Skim and cool.

CALF'S FOOT JELLY

4	calves' feet	2	cups sugar
5	qrts. cold water	1	pint sherry
*	whites and crushed shells of eggs	½	teaspoon nutmeg
*	juice of 3 limes	½	cup water
*	juice of 1 orange		

1. Clean feet well and put into a pan of cold water. Bring slowly to a boil and simmer for 5 hours. Set aside to cool overnight. In the morning skim jelly from the top and discard sediment on bottom.
2. Put on heat and melt slowly. Add egg whites beaten to a froth, the crushed shells, nutmeg, sugar and fruit juices. Boil hard for 20 minutes without stirring.
3. Add 1 cup of water and let come to a boil again. Reduce heat and let simmer covered for about 30 minutes.
4. Dip a flannel jelly bag into boiling water. Hang it up with a bowl underneath. Pour jelly into bag and let it drip. The bag must not be touched or jelly will cloud.
5. Turn jelly into a mould. Stir in wine and put in a cool place.

SEA GRAPE JELLY

7	lbs. sea grapes	*	sugar
7	pints water		

1. Add grapes to water and bring to a boil. Stir with a wooden spoon and crush fruit whilst stirring. Boil about 20 minutes.
2. Drip through a sieve without stirring.
3. Measure this juice and for every cup of liquid, add an equal amount of sugar.
4. Return sugar and liquid to heat and boil rapidly. Skim.
5. Boil until a little tested on a plate will jell.
6. Pour into jars, and cool before sealing.
7. Makes approx. 4-5 jars.

ORANGE JELLY AND GUAVA JELLY

7	lbs. sliced guavas or	7	pints water (boil 30 minutes)
7	cups diced oranges	*	sugar

1. These are made to the same formula as seagrape jelly (see above).
2. Strain and measure juice in each instance, and add an equal amount of sugar. Boil until liquid jells.
3. Pour into jars. Makes approx. 4-5 jars.

BLENDER GRAPEFRUIT MARMALADE

4	grapefruits	5	cups sugar
2	limes	1/8	teaspoon soda
1½ cups water		1	oz. gelatin powder

1. Lightly peel and seed grapefruit. Chop two and put into a blender with ½ cup water. Mince. Add soda to this and boil for 30 minutes.
2. Cut up remaining 2 grapefruits and limes discarding seeds. Add to ½ cup water and mince in blender. Add this to cooked mixture with rest of water and boil for 30 minutes.
3. Add sugar and stir and boil for 10-15 minutes, being careful to stir frequently to avoid burning and to melt sugar.
4. Add dissolved gelatin to marmalade when it has cooled slightly. Should make 4 jars.

ORANGE MARMALADE

4	large seville oranges	*	sugar
2	teaspoons salt		

1. Wash oranges and peel lightly. Cut into quarters, removing pips and pulp. Cover pips and pulp with water and let stand overnight. Slice (or cut with scissors) the peel very thinly and add a little salt. Cover with water and soak overnight.
2. The next morning bring peel to a boil and boil until tender. Strain liquid from pips and pulp and add to the fruit mixture. Measure this and add sugar equal to this quantity.
3. Boil up again, simmer and stir until sugar melts and liquid thickens. Be careful not to burn, so at this point cook on a low flame.
4. When mixture jells, skim and remove and pour into jars.

GUAVA CHEESE

*	ripe guavas (whatever number desired)	* sugar

1. Wash guavas, cover with water and boil until tender. Rub through a sieve, weigh the pulp, and add an equal quantity of sugar.
2. Boil until mixture shrinks from the sides of pot. Stir all the time to prevent burning.
3. When a little dropped in water forms a ball, pour into a shallow dish. Cool and cut into squares when firm.

LIME CURD

4	limes grated and juiced	4	ozs. butter
1	lb. granulated sugar	4	eggs beaten

1. Combine all ingredients in a double boiler and simmer until sugar dissolves and mixture is thick.
2. Makes 2 jars.

Desserts

DUCKANOO/ BLUE DRAWERS/ TIE LEAF

3 cups cornmeal	1 teaspoon vanilla
2 cups grated sweet potatoes	1 teaspoon mixed spice
1 cup flour	2 tablespoons melted margarine
1 teaspoon salt	1 cup grated coconut
2 cups coconut milk	¼ cup raisins
1½ cups brown sugar	

1. Combine cornmeal, sweet potatoes, flour, salt, mixed spice, margarine, grated coconut and raisins.
2. Sweeten coconut milk and sugar. Add vanilla.
3. Add milk mixture to cornmeal mixture and blend well.
4. Prepare banana leaves by cutting off centre vein and holding leaves over boiling water for about a minute.
5. Put half cup of mixture in banana leaves and fold sides into a packet.
6. Tie with the banana vein or twine.
7. Place packets in boiling water (enough to cover) and boil for thirty minutes.
8. Remove leaf covering to serve. Serves 8.

AMBROSIA

4 oranges peeled and sliced	½ cup pomegranate seeds
1 small shredded coconut	* sugar
4 tablespoons wine	

1. Pile fruit in alternate layers into a bowl, sprinkle with sugar, coconut and wine.
2. End with a layer of pomegranate seeds.

BANANAS IN BATTER

1	oz. sugar	½	cup rum
½	oz. butter	1	tablespoon sugar
9	tablespoons milk	1	teaspoon lime juice
1	teaspoon baking powder	8	ozs. flour
1	egg	*	oil
3	ripe bananas		

1. Peel bananas and cut into thick chunks.
2. Soak in rum, sugar and lime juice.
3. Mix remaining ingredients except the oil.
4. Dip banana chunks into the batter using a spoon. Fry lightly in hot oil.

RIPE BANANA PIE

2	sliced bananas	*	cherries
1	package lime jello - prepared as instructions	*	shredded coconut (optional)

1. Place sliced bananas in a prebaked pie shell.
2. Cover with cooked lime jello mixture. Chill.

BANANA PUDDING

6	ripe crushed bananas	¼	lb. sugar
3	tablespoons melted butter	3	beaten egg whites
1	glass white wine	*	vanilla to taste

1. Mix all together and beat until smooth.
2. Put into a soufflé dish, and bake in a 325°F oven until puffy and golden brown on top.
3. Serve at once. The yolk may be used to make a sauce to serve with the pudding.
4. Decorate with cherries and shredded coconut.

CASHEW NUT ICE CREAM

		1	qrt. vanilla ice cream
1	cup grape juice	*	pinch ginger powder
½	cup chopped cashew nuts		

1. Mix the juice, nuts and ginger into the ice cream.
2. Refreeze for about 2 hours.

COCONUT CREAM PIE

1½	cups milk	1	teaspoon vanilla and a pinch of salt
¾	cup grated coconut	2	cups flour
3	eggs, separated	1	cup margarine
4	tablespoons sugar	4	tablespoons ice water - salt to taste

1. Heat milk and set aside, beat yolks and add sugar, vanilla, salt and coconut.
2. Stir in heated milk and fold in stiffly beaten egg whites.
3. Mix together flour, margarine, water and salt to form a dough.
4. Roll out and line a pie dish. Prick the bottom.
5. Pour in filling and bake for 50 minutes in a 350°F oven.

COCONUT GIZZADAS

1	lb. brown sugar	2	cups flour
¼	pt. water	¼	teaspoon salt
1	grated coconut	¼	cup margarine
½	teaspoon nutmeg	*	iced water to blend

1. Make a syrup of sugar and water. Add coconut and nutmeg. Mix well.
2. Cool and fill pastry, shells made as follows.
3. Mix flour and salt, cut in margarine and water.
4. Roll out and cut into circles, mould into cases and pinch up edges.
5. Fill with mixture and bake in a 400°F oven until pastry shells are golden brown.

COCONUT MOULD

3	cups coconut cream	1	tablespoon gelatin powder
1	tin condensed milk	¼	cup warm water

1. Dissolve gelatin in warm water. Mix with coconut cream and condensed milk.
2. Heat through to melt gelatin, but do not boil or mixture will curdle.
3. Cool and chill.

PER PERSON

1	egg	1	tablespoon black coffee
1	oz. plain chocolate	1	tablespoon rum

1. Melt chocolate over low heat.
2. Separate eggs, reserving whites, beat yolks and stir into melted chocolate mixed with coffee and rum.
3. Whip egg whites and fold into mixture. Put into individual glasses and chill.

TROPICAL FRUIT SALAD

1 ripe pineapple or melon
  variety of diced fruits, as desired

* brandy, optional

1. Cut off the top of a ripe pineapple or use a melon cut into 2 parts. Scoop out flesh and mix with diced fruits - as many varieties as desired.
2. Toss with 2 tablespoons brandy if desired.
3. Return to shell and chill. Fresh lychee and mangoes can be added for a surprise. Both these fruits are obtainable in the Castleton area.

GUAVA MOUSSE

2 tablespoons water
1 cup whipped cream

1 cup tinned guava nectar
1 tablespoon gelatin powder

1. Dissolve gelatin in water and add to guava nectar.
2. Heat slowly to melt gelatin.
3. Cool slightly before adding the whipped cream.
4. Set in individual glasses. Chill to serve.

GUAVA PIE

CRUST
1½ cups flour
2 tablespoons sugar
1¼ teaspoons baking powder

3 tablespoons butter
¾ cup milk
* a pinch of salt

1. Mix flour, sugar, baking powder and salt.
2. Cut butter into this and blend until mixture looks like cornmeal. Stir in milk.
3. Knead on a floured board for 1 minute. Divide dough into 2 balls.
4. Roll out bottom crust, cut and fit into a greased pie dish. Put in filling of guava slices with some syrup.
5. Cover with remaining dough. Brush over with milk and make one or two slits in the pastry.
6. Bake in a 350°F oven for about 30 minutes.

FILLING
ripe guavas (when in season)
or use tinned guavas

* water
* sugar

1. Peel fresh guavas, cut in half and scoop out seeds.
2. Cover with water, add sugar and boil slowly until fruit is tender and a syrup has formed. Fill crust.

LIME PIE

2 egg yolks
4 ozs. condensed milk
¾ cup lime juice
* salt

6 tablespoons sugar
3 egg whites
1 baked pie shell

1. Beat yolks, stir in milk and add lime juice gradually. Beat well.
2. Whip egg whites with a pinch of salt and fold into mixture.
3. Pour into a baked pie shell and cover with meringue made with 3 stiffly beaten whites and 6 tablespoons sugar.
4. Bake in a preheated oven for 10 minutes - or until meringue is a golden colour.

MAMMEE APPLE PIE

1 mammee apple
1 8" baked pie shell
2 tablespoons brown sugar

1 cup water
1 tablespoon lime juice
½ teaspoon mixed spices

1. Make a syrup with sugar, water and lime juice.
2. Peel and scrape the fruit, slice and simmer gently in the syrup until tender.
3. Fill the pre-baked crust and sprinkle with spices.
4. Chill and serve with cream - or coconut cream if desired.

PIE CRUST
8 ozs. flour
4 ozs. margarine

* pinch of salt
* coldwater

1. Combine flour, margarine and salt. Add 2-3 tablespoons cold water to make a soft dough.
2. Roll out pastry larger than pie dish.
3. Cut to fit, lapping over dish edge slightly.
4. Cut a border and press it around the dampened edges of dish.
5. Bake for ½ hour in 350°F oven. Allow to cool before filling.

BOMBAY MANGO FOOL

6 Bombay mangoes
6 teaspoons condensed milk
1 cup light cream

1 teaspoon lime juice
* nutmeg

1. Peel mangoes, slice flesh off seeds and put through a blender.
2. Add milk, cream, lime juice and nutmeg.
3. Stir well and chill.

BOMBAY MANGO SPECIAL

1   mango per person

1.   Halve the mangoes and take out the seeds.
2.   Fill cavities with vanilla ice cream.

NASEBERRY PANCAKES

1   cup milk
1   egg
1   egg yolk
1   tablespoon sugar

4   ozs. flour
1   tablespoon butter
5   naseberries

1.   Combine first 6 ingredients to make a batter. Add the naseberries, peeled and crushed.
2.   Mix well and drop by the spoonful onto a hot, greased fry pan. Brown on both sides.
3.   Serve with butter or syrup.

ORANGE ICE BOX DESSERT

2   cups milk
2   tablespoons cornstarch
1   cup sugar
4   egg yolks
1   tablespoon gelatin

2   tablespoons cold water
¾   cup orange juice
1   teaspoon orange rind
1   pt. whipped cream
*   sponge cake slices

1.   Heat milk in double boiler. Mix cornstarch, sugar and yolks and pour into warm milk. Cook slowly for 10 minutes.
2.   Dissolve gelatin into warm water and add juice and rind. Place in refrigerator to chill and thicken.
3.   Line a spring form pan with slices of sponge cake. Pour mixture over this and chill.
4.   Just before serving top with some whipped cream.

ORANGE SORBET

1½ pts. water
5   ozs. Sugar
4   oranges

1   lime
1   glass white wine
1   egg white

1.   Bring the sugar and water to a boil, dissolve and reduce.
2.   Add the grated rind of 1 orange, and the juice of 4 oranges and 1 lime.
3.   Bring to a boil, strain and cool.
4.   Semi-freeze. Whisk egg white briskly and add -along with wine to mixture.
5.   Freeze until mushy and serve in parfait glasses.

OTAHEITE PUDDING

ripe otaheite apples   1   teaspoon spice
¾   cup sugar   1   teaspoon baking powder
2   tablespoons butter or margarine

1. Peel and slice apples. Sprinkle sugar in a greased dish and dot with butter and spice.
2. Arrange apple slices on top.
3. Pour naseberry batter over the slices, or use other batter, adding 1 tsp. of baking powder.
4. Bake at 350°F for 35 minutes.

PICKNEY'S SWEET

½   jar of strawberry jam   *   whipped cream and chopped nuts
*   a little water

1. Heat jam with water to thin slightly.
2. Pour into glasses.
3. Cool and top with whipped cream and chopped nuts.

RUM COFFEE JELLY

2   tablespoons gelatin   3   tablespoons rum
2   cups of hot strong coffee   2   cups sour cream
½   cup sugar   1   cup brown sugar
2   tablespoons lime juice   ½   teaspoon cinnamon

1. Soften gelatin in ½ cup of cold water.
2. Add hot coffee and sugar and stir until gelatin is dissolved. Add lime juice and rum.
3. Pour into an 8" dish and chill until firm. Cut into cubes and serve a sauce made by beating together sour cream, sugar and cinnamon until sugar dissolves.

CORNMEAL MUFFINS

1   cup cornmeal   ½   cup sugar
1¼   cups flour   1   egg
2   teaspoons baking powder   1 cup milk
½   teaspoon salt   ¾ cup raisins
½   cup butter

1. In a large bowl, stir together flour, cornmeal, baking powder and salt.
2. In a separate bowl, cream butter and sugar until fluffy.
3. Then beat in egg and milk.
4. Add liquid mix to dry mix and put in raisins.
5. Pour batter into a greased muffin tin, leaving space for the muffins to rise.
6. Bake at 400°F for 20 minutes or until tops are springy to the touch.

CORNMEAL PUDDING

2 cups coconut milk
4 cups water
½ cup margarine
½ cup raisins
2 cups brown sugar
3 cups cornmeal

½ cup flour
½ tablespoon cinnamon
1½ teaspoons salt
2 teaspoons vanilla
2½ cups milk

FOR SOFT TOP
1 cup coconut milk
½ cup brown sugar

½ teaspoon cinnamon

1. Put coconut milk, water, margarine, raisins and sugar to boil.
2. Combine cornmeal, flour, cinnamon, nutmeg, salt and vanilla and add 2½ cups milk to soften.
3. Add to the boiling liquid and stir briskly.
4. Lower flame and boil for ten minutes stirring continuously.
5. Pour into a greased baking tin, then top mixture of coconut milk, sugar and cinnamon.
6. Bake at 350°F in a preheated oven for about 55-60 minutes.
7. Remove from oven, cool and serve. Maybe served with rum sauce (See Dressings & Sauces).

A TASTY, LOW-CHOLESTEROL RECIPE FOR PASTRY

1 cup flour
½ teaspoon salt
¼ cup vegetable oil

2 tablespoons skim milk (use instant) powder mixed in water

1. Mix flour and salt. Combine oil and milk and pour over flour.
2. Stir with a fork till smooth.
3. Shape into a ball, flatten and wrap with a sheet of waxed paper. Chill.
4. Peel off the paper and roll out. Use as desired.

SWEET POTATO PUDDING

2 lbs. sweet potato
¼ lb. yam
½ cup flour
¼ lb. raisins
1 teaspoon baking powder
½ tin evaporated milk

5 cups coconut milk
2 teaspoons vanilla
½ teaspoon nutmeg
½ teaspoon salt
¼ cup rum
¼ oz. butter

1. Preheat oven to 350°F.
2. Mix grated potato, yam, flour, raisins and baking powder.
3. Mix evaporated milk, coconut milk, sugar, vanilla, nutmeg, salt, rum and butter.
4. Pour milk mixture into potato mixture. Beat until smooth.
5. Pour into a greased 9 inch tin and settle mixture for about ½ hour.
6. Bake at 350°F for about 1½ hours until set. Serve hot or cold.

Cakes & Breads

BASIC BREAD DOUGH

2½ cups flour	2 tablespoons melted butter
1 teaspoon dry yeast	5 tablespoons cold milk
½ cup warm water	1 egg beaten into 1 tablespoon milk
* pinch of salt	2 tablespoons flour

1. Sift flour and salt. Dissolve yeast in a cup of warm water. Combine with butter and milk. Cover bowl and set aside to rise for 2 hours.
2. Put 2 tablespoons flour on table and pat dough to ½" thickness. Cut dough into 2 pieces and roll from corner to corner like a jelly roll.
3. Brush with egg and milk and slash surface at intervals. Place in bread loaf pans and bake 15 minutes in a fast oven, then lower to 350°F and bake 15 minutes more.

BANANA BREAD

1 cup sugar	1 unbeaten egg
¼ cup margarine or butter	1 teaspoon baking powder
3 crushed, ripe bananas	½ teaspoon soda
2 cups flour	* vanilla flavouring

1. Cream sugar and butter. Add bananas and mix well. Add egg and dry ingredients and vanilla. Beat well.
2. Bake in a greased, paper lined loaf tin at 350°F for 50 minutes. This freezes well.

EGG BREAD

2 teaspoons sugar	4 cups flour
2 eggs (beaten)	1 cup warm water
1 egg yolk	1 tablespoon oil
1 pk. yeast	

1. Soak yeast in warm water for 5 minutes. Sift flour, salt and sugar together. Add 1 ½ cups flour to the yeast and beat. Cover and allow to rise about 30 minutes.
2. Add the 2 eggs and remaining flour and oil to dough. Knead. Place in a bowl to rise for 2 hours.
3. Knead dough again. Divide into 3 strands and braid, turning ends under. Place on a greased sheet and let rise for 1 hour.
4. Preheat 400°F. Brush the top with egg yolk. Bake for 10-15 minutes. Reduce oven to 350°F and bake 30 minutes. Bread should be golden brown on top.

ORANGE BREAD

1   cup minced orange peel
1   cup orange juice
2½ cups of sugar
1   beaten egg
3½ cups flour

1   cup milk
½   teaspoon melted butter
2   teaspoons baking powder
*   pinch of salt

1. Combine orange peel and juice and boil until peel is tender. Add 1½ cups sugar, and boil slowly until thick and syrupy. Cool.
2. Mix egg, 1 cup sugar, butter and milk. Sift flour with baking powder and salt. Add mixture and stir. Add orange mixture to dough and blend well.
3. Pour into 2 loaf tins which have been greased and floured. Bake at 350°F for 40 minutes. This is good toasted with cheese spread.

BAKING POWDER BISCUITS

2   cups flour
2½ teaspoons baking powder
⅓ cup margarine

¾   cup milk
*   salt

1. Sift together flour and baking powder. Cut margarine into the flour mixture with a fork. Add milk and salt. Knead and roll out to ½" thickness.
2. Cut into circles and bake on an ungreased sheet for 15 minutes in a hot oven, 400-450°F.

CARROT CAKE

1   lb. carrots grated
2   cups granulated sugar
2   cups corn oil
6   eggs
3   cups flour
1   teaspoon ginger
½   teaspoon salt

2   teaspoons baking powder
1   teaspoon baking soda
1   cup walnuts
1   cup mixed fruit
1   cup raisins
*   Vanilla, almond essence and cinnamon to flavour

1. Preheat oven to 350°F.
2. Grease 10 inch pan.
3. Sift all dry ingredients (Flour, baking powder, baking soda, sugar, salt).
4. Beat eggs while adding oil. Fold in dry mixture and remainder of ingredients.
5. Pour in baking pan and bake for approximately one hour or until toothpick comes out clean.

BANANA MUFFINS

6½ ozs. flour
1 tablespoon corn flour
2 ozs. butter
3 ozs. sugar

1 egg
3 crushed bananas
1 teaspoon baking powder
½ teaspoon soda and a pinch of salt

1. Sift together flour, cornflour, baking powder, soda and salt.
2. Cream butter and sugar. Beat egg and mix into creamed mixture.
3. Add dry ingredients and crushed bananas alternately. Do hot beat, but mix in well.
4. Bake in greased muffin containers in 400°F oven for 20 minutes.

BAPS

1 lb. flour
½ teaspoon salt
2 ozs. margarine

1 teaspoon sugar
½ pt. of warm milk
2 teaspoons yeast powder

1. Sift together, flour, cornflour, baking powder, soda and salt. Cream butter and sugar.
2. Beat egg and mix into creamed mixture.
3. Add dry ingredients and crushed bananas alternately. Do hot beat, but mix in well. Bake in greased muffin containers in 400°F oven for 20 minutes.

BULLAS

3 cups flour
8 ozs. brown sugar
2 ozs. melted butter

2 ozs. water
1 teaspoon baking powder

1. Make a syrup of water and sugar. Sift together dry ingredients and add syrup and melted butter.
2. Turn on to a floured board and pat into ¼ inch thickness.
3. Cut into circles. Place on a greased tin and bake for 20 minutes in a 400°F oven.

CASSAVA BAMMY

2 lbs. sweet cassavas

1. Scrape the cassava and grate. Squeeze out the juice, letting the flour remain. Rub through this flour to remove all lumps.
2. Put a thick-bottomed pan over a low heat and when hot, pour in the cassava flour. When it sets at the bottom, turn over and let the other side set. Scrape to remove any scorching.
3. Bammies may be moistened with a little milk and baked in an oven or browned under grill, or fry them in a pan with a little bacon fat. Each bammy should be about 5' - 6' in diameter and about ½-¾ inch thick.

CASSAVA PUFFS

1 lb. sweet cassava
1 tablespoon margarine
1 beaten egg

1 teaspoon baking powder
1 teaspoon salt

1. Peel cassavas and boil until tender with some salt. Crush whilst still hot. Add margarine, baking powder and beaten egg and beat.
2. Drop by spoonfuls into muffin tins which have been greased. Bake for 15 minutes in hot oven. Puffs may also be fried.

A JAMAICAN BUN

1 lb. flour
2 ozs. butter
2 ozs. margarine
2 ozs. raisins
2 ozs. mixed peel
2 eggs

6 ozs. currants
½ lb. brown sugar
½ teaspoon nutmeg
½ teaspoon baking powder
* enough milk to make a batter

1. Blend butter and margarine into flour. Add baking powder, sugar and nutmeg.
2. Add fruit to flour.
3. Beat the eggs and pour into the dry mixture adding enough milk to make a batter.
4. Pour into a greased loaf in and bake 1½ hours in a slow oven about 300°.
5. Chopped cherries and some lime rind may be added to the mixture if desired.

OR

EASTER SPICE BUNS

3 cups flour
¼ tsp. baking powder
1 tbsp. baking soda
2 cups hot water
1½ cups brown sugar
4 tbsp. margarine
1 lb. raisins
¼ lb. mixed dried fruit

¼ tsp. molasses
¼ tsp. salt
1 tsp. cinnamon
1 tsp. nutmeg
½ tsp. ground allspice
3 tbsp. water
3 tbsp. sugar

1. Preheat oven to 325°F.
2. In a large bowl, combine flour, baking powder, and baking soda.
3. In a medium saucepan, bring water to a boil.
4. Add sugar, stirring until dissolved.
5. Lower heat; add margarine, raisins, mixed fruit, molasses, salt, and spices.
6. Let simmer for 10 minutes.
7. Remove from heat and let cool.
8. Add cooled liquid to flour mixture. Stir and blend, but do not over mix.
9. To glaze buns before baking, combine water and sugar and brush mixture onto buns.
10. Pour batter into a 5" x 9" greased loaf pan.
11. Bake for 1 to 1½ hours.

COCONUT LOAF CAKE

½ cup butter	2 eggs
1½ cups sugar	4 teaspoons baking powder
2²/₃ cups flour	1 cup grated coconut
¾ cup milk	1 teaspoon vanilla

1. Cream butter and ½ of the sugar.
2. Beat eggs with rest of sugar and combine the mixture.
3. Mix in flour and baking powder adding milk alternately with the dry ingredients.
4. Add coconut and vanilla.
5. Bake 1 hour in a 350°F oven.

GUAVA LAYER CAKE

½ lb. margarine	2 teaspoons baking powder
1 cup sugar	¼ teaspoon nutmeg
2 eggs	½ teaspoon vanilla
2 cups flour	* stewed guava slices, or use tinned
1 cup milk	

1. Cream margarine, sugar and eggs. Beat well.
2. Add flour, baking powder and nutmeg. Pour in milk to which vanilla has been added.
3. Bake in two 9" layer tins for 30 minutes in a 350°F oven.
4. Cool and remove from pans. Spread guava slices between the layers.
5. Sprinkle sugar lightly on top. Stewed mangoes may be used in the same manner.

ORANGE CAKE

3 oranges	½ teaspoon soda and a tip of salt
2 eggs	1 cup butter
¾ cup sugar	¼ cup grated orange rind
2 cups flour	

1. Squeeze juice from oranges to make 1 cup and reserve.
2. Cream butter and sugar and add eggs one at a time, beating continuously.
3. Add flour, salt and soda, which have been sifted together.
4. Continue to beat the mixture. Add ¼ cup of orange rind and the juice.
5. Pour into a greased 13" x 9" pan and bake in a moderate oven until firm.

RUM CAKE

½ cup butter
1 cup sugar
3 beaten eggs
¼ teaspoon salt
½ teaspoon baking powder
3 cups flour
* mixed spices

¼ cup milk
¼ cup molasses
2 cups peanuts (crushed)
1 lb. raisins
½ cup rum
* pinch of soda

1. Cream butter, sugar and eggs.
2. Mix flour, baking powder, salt and spices. Add this to butter mixture and blend.
3. Add milk, soda and molasses, and add lastly crushed nuts, raisins and rum.
4. Bake in a loaf tin 300°F for 2 hours.

KATIE'S SHORT BREAD

1 oz. sugar
4 ozs. butter

2½ ozs. flour
2½ ozs. cornflour (cornstarch)

1. Cream butter and sugar. Add flour and cornflour and blend thoroughly.
2. Put through a cookie tube or drop by spoonfuls onto a greased sheet.
3. Bake for 10 minutes in a 375°F oven. Sprinkle with sugar.

COCONUT COOKIES

¾ cup sugar
¼ lb. butter
1½ cups flour

1 tsp. baking powder
1½ cups grated coconut
1 beaten egg

1. Cream butter and sugar. Add flour and baking powder.
2. Mix. well then add grated coconut and egg.
3. Mix to a paste. Drop onto a greased cookie sheet by teaspoonsful.
4. Bake at 350°F for 15 minutes. Makes approx. 2 doz.

GUAVA JELLY COOKIES

4 ozs. butter
2 ozs. sugar
1 egg yolk
½ teaspoon vanilla
4 ozs. flour

1 egg white
3 tablespoons chopped nuts
3 tablespoons guava jelly
* pinch of salt

1. Cream butter and sugar and beat in yolk and vanilla. Combine flour and salt and add to mixture.
2. Divide and shape into balls. Roll in egg white and then in nuts. Press a hole into each cookie and insert guava jelly.
3. Bake with jelly uppermost, on a sheet for 20 minutes in a moderate oven. Makes approx.1 doz.

SWEET POTATO COOKIES

1½ cups flour	1 cup crushed, boiled, sweet potato
2 tablespoons brown sugar	½ cup of milk
4 teaspoons baking powder	* cinnamon
5 tablespoons butter	

1. Combine all but milk and potatoes and mix until crumbly. Stir in crushed potatoes and milk.
2. Spoon batter on to a sheet.
3. Bake in a quick oven.
4. Split and serve with honey and butter. Makes approx. 1 doz.

CORN BREAD

1 cup cornmeal	½ teaspoon salt
1 cup flour	½ cup milk or coconut milk
2 tablespoons sugar	2 eggs beaten
4 tablespoons baking powder	¼ cup oil

1. Preheat oven to 220°F.
2. Grease baking pan.
3. Mix together cornmeal, flour, sugar and salt.
4. Whisk together beaten eggs and coconut milk.
5. Add to this the dry ingredients and stir, blending well.
6. Add oil and bake for 25 minutes.

Beverages

MATRIMONY

3	star apples	4	tablespoons condensed milk
2	oranges	*	nutmeg

1. Remove star apple pulp. Peel orange and remove sections, discarding seeds.
2. Mix together, sweeten with condensed milk, and flavour with grated nutmeg. Chill.

NASEBERRY NECTAR

8	naseberries peeled and seeded	1	cup water
1	cup sugar	*	juice of 1 orange

Put all ingredients through a blender, strain and serve chilled.

PLANTATION RUM PUNCH

3	ozs. any rum	1	teaspoon honey
1	oz. lime juice	*	nutmeg

Mix together and pour over cracked ice. Add a sprinkle of nutmeg.

SORREL APPETIZER

1	lb. prepared sorrel	6	pints boiling water
2	ozs. grated green ginger		

1. Mix ingredients together, cover and leave overnight.
2. Strain and add rum and sugar to taste.
3. Serve over crushed ice.

SOURSOP PUNCH

1	ripe soursop	*	condensed milk to taste
4	glasses water	*	vanilla or rum to flavour

1. Peel and crush soursop, removing seeds.
2. Stir in water and strain.
3. Add milk and flavouring. Serve ice cold.

STARAPPLE APPETIZER

6	starapples (use pulp only)	2	teaspoons lime juice
2	tablespoons rum	*	angostura bitters
2	tablespoons sugar		

1. Cut starapples in half, remove pulp and mix with rum, sugar and lime juice.
2. Add a few drops of angostura bitters. Serve chilled in fruit glasses.

For a full range of non-alcoholic beverages see CARIBBEAN COCKTAILS & MIXED DRINKS by Mike Henry

BANANA MILK-SHAKE

2	ripe bananas	1	scoop vanilla ice cream
1	pint milk (cold)	½	teaspoon vanilla

1. Puree the bananas in a blender. Add the cold milk, ice cream and vanilla.
2. Blend well and serve in two tall glasses with straws.
3. If the milk shake is very thick, it can be served over cracked ice.

CHRISTMAS CITRUS PUNCH

6	cups grapefruit juice	¾	cup honey (or to taste)
5	cups ortanique juice	1	whole orange, unpeeled
3	cups orange juice	12	cloves
2	bottles soda water		

1. Stick the cloves into the orange and bake in a warm oven until hard. Put the honey into a large bowl and add the fruit juices gradually, stirring so that the honey is completely dissolved. Add the baked orange. Allow the mixture to stand for two hours at least.
2. When ready to serve, place a block of ice in a large bowl and pour the punch over it. Use a ladle to pour the punch over the ice repeatedly until it is completely chilled. Add the soda water and serve.
3. Rum can be added to this punch while it is standing. It can also be garnished with sprigs of mint.

JAMAICAN GINGER BEER

¼ lb. root ginger
2   lbs. sugar
1   oz. yeast

1   lime
½   oz. cream of tartar
6   quarts boiling water

1. Grate ginger and place in a large bowl. Add the lime thinly sliced and cream of tartar. Pour the boiling water over all and allow to stand.

2. In a separate bowl, mix yeast with one cup sugar. Add ½ cup luke warm water to make a smooth paste.

3. When the ginger mixture is luke warm, add the yeast and sugar. Stir well. Cover. Let stand for 2-3 days. Skim and strain, then add the sugar, stirring well until it is dissolved.

4. Pour into bottles and let the ginger beer stand at room temperature for three or four days more. Serve chilled. Rum can be added at the bottling stage, if desired.

MENUS

BRUNCH

1.   Hot Buttered Rum or Carrot Punch *
    Jerk Pork Snacks
    Pepper Shrimps
    Banana Muffins
    Bombay Mango Fool

2.   Boo Boo's Special *
    Curried Codfish
    Fruited Cabbage
    Baps
    Katie's Shortbread
    Coffee a la Mike

3.   Policeman Glow *
    Ackee & Saltfish
    Stuffed Breadfruit
    Callaloo Salad
    Matrimony

4.   Bloody Mary *
    Escoveitch of Fish (Grouper)
    Bammy
    Naseberry Pancakes served with syrup
    and butter, or orange jelly
    Jamaican Coffee

5.   Coffee Coconut *
    Crab Fritters
    Cucumber and Sour Cream Salad garnished
    with sweet peppers
    Pumpkin Bread served with tomato jam
    Tropical Fruit Salad

6.   Sour-Sop Punch
Liver with sweet pepper
Cassava Puffs served with pineapple jam
Ambrosia
Coffee a la Blue Mountain

7.   Naked Lady or Hot Barbados Rum
Naseberry Nectar
Fresh Fruit Plate
Pepper Shrimps
Ackee with Cheese
Jamaican Bun

LUNCH

1.   Hot Flashes *
Jamaica Fish Pie
Pumpkin Salad garnished with sweet pepper rings and parsley
Otaheite Pudding

2.   Pineapple Cocktails *
Jamaica Fish Tea
Broad Bean Salad
Beef & Mango in beer
Yam Casserole
Sliced Tomatoes
Orange Sorbet

3.   Air Conditioner*
Jamaica Pepper Pot Soup
Chicken Salad
Sweet Pepper Salad
Pumpkin Bread
Coconut Mould

4.   Banana Punch*
Coco Soup
Tropical Chicken
String Bean Salad
Rum Coffee Jelly

5.   Woodpecker
       Jamaican Salad
       Curried Goat with rice
       Mammee Apple Pie

6.   Special Jamaican Rum Punch (hot)*
       Fish Chowder
       Poor Man's Fillet
       Rice & Peas
       Carrot & Raisin Salad
       Guava Mousse

7.   Spanish Town *
       Pumpkin Soup
       Marinated Pork Chops
       Cho Cho Salad
       Breadfruit Salad
       Coconut Cream Pie

DINNER

1.   Desperate Virgin *
       Grapefruit with shrimp & sour cream
       Jamaican Salad
       Conch Soup
       Salmi of Duck
       Pumpkin Puff
       Chochos baked with cheese
       Guava Layer Cake

2.   Suffering Bastard*
       or Starapple Appetizer
       Avocado & Grapefruit Salad
       Gungo Pea Soup
       Pork Chops with Pineapple
       Baked Sweet Potatoes
       Guava Mousse

3.   Clarendon Cocktail*
       Ackee Salad
       Red Pea Soup
       Dumperpumpkin with rice
       Onion Salad
       Guava Pie

4.   Frozen Daiquiri (Stella's Joy)*
     Lobster Salad
     Barbecued Lamb Chops
     Callaloo Bake
     Mint Glazed Carrots
     Orange Ice Box Dessert

5.   Pineapple Caribbean *
     Conch Salad
     Barbecued Chicken
     Corn Fritters
     Cauliflower Custard
     Banana Pudding

6.   Dry Martini *
     Shrimp Salad with coconut cream
     Cold Thick Cucumber Soup
     Deboned Stuffed Leg of Kid with browned
     potatoes
     Egg Plant with Cheese & tomatoes
     Carrot Ambrosia
     Ripe banana pie

7.   West Indian Punch *
     Tropical Salad
     ChoCho Puree
     King Fish Fillets
     Yam Casserole
     Beans in sour cream sauce
     Lime Pie

     * See "Caribbean Cocktails" by Mike Henry

GLOSSARY OF COOKING TERMS

BAIN MARIE	A French cooking utensil similar to a double boiler used to cook over boiling water	Cut in	To mix batter or margarine with dry ingredients, with a pastry blender, knives or fork
Bake	To cook by dry heat, usually in an oven	DEBONE	To remove bones from meat, poultry, game and fish
Barbecue	Generally refers to food cooked outdoors over art open fire with a spicy sauce	Deep Fry	To cook in deep hot fat or oil which covers the food until crisp and golden
Baste	To brush or spoon liquid over food while cooking, to keep it moist	Dice	To cut into small cubes
		Disjoint	To separate the joints - of poultry etc.
Batter	Any combination which includes flour, milk, butter, eggs or the like for pancakes, coating, dipping etc.	Dot	To scatter small bits of butter or margarine over surface of food
Beat	To mix with a whisk beater or spoon so as to make the mixture smooth	FLAME	To spoon alcoholic fluid over and ignite, to warm the alcohol, and pour flaming over food
Blanch	To heat in boiling water or steam for a short period only to loosen skin, remove colour or set colour	Fold in	To use a spoon in a gentle rolling circular action as a means of combining ingredients
Blend	To mix two or more ingredients thoroughly	Fry	To cook in hot fat using moderate to high heat
Boil	To cook in any liquid at boiling point		
		GHEE	Clarified butter, used in curries
CHILL	To place in refrigerator until cold	Glaze	A thin coating of beaten egg-milk, syrup or aspic which is brushed over pastry, fruits, ham chicken etc.
Coat	To cover entire surface of food with flour, breadcrumbs, or batter		
Cream	To combine butter or other shortening with sugar using a wooden spoon or mixer until light and fluffy	Grate	To rub food against a grater to form small particles
		Grill	To cook by direct heat either over a charcoal fire or under a gas or electric grill unit
Croutons	Small cubes of fried bread		

JULIENNE	A term for foods cut into thin strips like matches		Sauté	To fry lightly in a small amount of fat turning and stirring frequently
KNEAD	To work dough with hands until it is of the desired elasticity or consistency		Scald	To pour boiling water over foods, or bring to boiling
MARINADE	Liquid used for seasoning by soaking usually a mixture of oil, wine and seasonings		Score	To cut narrow gashes on the surface of foods
			Shred	To cut into fine strips
Marinate	To soak in a marinade to soften or add flavour		Simmer	To cook in liquid just below boiling point
PARBOIL	To boil until partly cooked		Skim	To remove foam, fat or solid substances from the surface of a cooking mixture.
Pate	A highly seasoned meat paste			
Pit	To remove pit-stone or seed-from fruit		Sliver	To cut into long thin strips
Poach	To cook gently in simmering liquid		Steam	To cook in vapour rising from boiling water
Pound	To reduce to small particles or a paste, using a pestle and mortar		Stew	A long slow method of cooking in liquid in a covered pan, to tenderize tough meats.
Preheat	To turn over to a selected temperature 10 minutes before it is needed		Stir	To blend ingredients with a circular motion
Puree	To press through a fine sieve or put through a food blender to produce a smooth mixture		Stock	A liquid containing the flavours, extracts, and nutrients of bones - meat fish or vegetables, in which they are cooked
REDUCE	To cook over a high heat, uncovered until it is reduced to desired consistency		TOAST	To brown in a toaster, or oven
			Toss	To mix lightly, using a fork and a spoon - i.e. salads chiefly
Roast	To cook meat by dry heat in the oven or on a spit			
Roux	A mixture of fat and flour cooked slowly, stirring frequently - used to thicken sauces soups etc.		WHIP	To beat rapidly with hand or electric beater or wire whisk
SALMI	A hash - usually of duck			

35 USEFUL COOKING & HOUSEHOLD HINTS

1/3 to 1/2 teaspoon of dried herbs = 1 tablespoon fresh herbs.

Rub ½ lime on your hands or cutting board to remove onion, garlic or fish odours.

To avoid trouble with weevils, keep flour or cornmeal in a glass jar or plastic container in the refrigerator.

1 tablespoon oil in water for boiling pastas (macaroni etc.) prevents it from sticking together.

1 lb. coffee brews 40 cups.

For a tender pie crust use less water than is called for.

Dip knife in hot water to slice hard boiled eggs.

1 cup macaroni makes 2 cups of cooked macaroni.

Freeze left over coffee in an ice cube tray. When used to chill iced coffee, the cubes will not dilute the coffee.

Parsley rinsed in hot water instead of cold retains more flavour.

Brown sugar will not become lumpy if stored in a jar with a piece of blotting paper fitted to the inside of the jar lid.

If food boils over in the oven, cover with salt to prevent smoking and excessive odour.

Add diced crisp bacon and a dash of nutmeg to cauliflower or cabbage for a gourmet touch.

To keep kettles clean, fill with cold water, add some ammonia and bring to a boil. Rinse well.

Gas ovens must be wiped clean before oven is cold. Racks and shelves must be washed with hot water and washing soda.

Wash pewter with hot water and soap, polish will scratch the surface.

Mildew stains can be removed by soaking overnight in sour milk. Dry in the sun without rinsing. Repeat process if necessary.

To remove a scorch, spread a paste of starch and cold water over the mark. Dry in sun and brush off.

Wash glass windows with crumpled newspaper dipped in cold water, to which a few drops of ammonia has been added.

For wood worms - apply kerosene oil with a brush to the infected area daily for 10 days.

To stop doors creaking rub hinges with soap.

Rust marks can be removed from steel by rubbing with a cut onion.

When washing thermos flasks, add a little vinegar to the water. It removes the musty smell. Do not cork flasks when storing.

To remove stains from china use a rag dipped in cold water and salt.

Before baking, have ingredients at room temperature.

To chop sticky dried fruits, heat knife before using.

To prepare nuts, first blanch. Cover with cold water and bring to the boil. Let soak until wrinkled then slip the skin off between the fingers.

Parsley freezes well. Cut stems and place bunch in a plastic bag. Thaws easily.

Tear lettuce into pieces instead of cutting to prevent browning.

It is a good idea to make stock from left over bones and keep in the freezer to enhance soups and sauces.

Soak tarnished silver in hot water and ammonia - 1 tablespoon ammonia to 1 quart water.

Sour milk can be made by adding two teaspoons of lime juice to a cup of warm milk, which will curdle.

Moulds should be oiled before they are filled. Custards baked in hot water should be removed and left to stand for 5 minutes to settle before unmoulding. Run knife around the edge. Place a plate over the mould, invert the plate and mould and lift off.

As soon as vegetables are tender drain and plunge into cold water. This sets the colour. Vegetables may be stored and reheated when needed.

Whip cream in a large bowl set in ice. If no cream is available, place a tin of evaporated milk in the freezer for about one hour and then proceed to whip as for cream. To sweeten, use icing sugar, which is preferred to granulated sugar.

TABLE OF MEASUREMENTS AND MISCELLANEOUS EQUIVALENTS

Dash	=	Less than 1/8 teaspoon		
3 teaspoons	=	Tablespoon	=	15 ml
4 tablespoons	=	¼ cup	=	60 ml
8 tablespoons	=	½ cup	=	120ml
16 tablespoons	=	1 cup	=	240 ml
1 cup	=	½ pint	=	240 ml
2 cups	=	1 pint	=	480 ml
4 cups	=	1 quart	=	960 ml or .95 litres
2 liquid cups	=	1 lb.		
2 pints	=	1 quart	=	960 ml or .95 litres
4 quarts	=	1 gallon	=	3.8 litres
1 fluid ounce	=	2 tablespoons	=	30 ml
8 fluid ounces	=	1 cup	=	240 ml
16 ounces	=	1 pound =		480 ml
1 lb. butter	=	2 cups	=	454 grams
1 carrot	=	½ cup chopped		
¼ lb. cheese	=	1 cup grated		
1 envelope gelatin	=	1 tablespoon		
1 teaspoon dried herbs	=	1 tablespoon fresh		
juice of 1 lime	=	1 tablespoon		
1 medium onion	=	¾ cup chopped		
1 medium potato	=	¼ cup chopped		
1 pk. dry yeast	=	¾ oz.	=	21 grams

SOME SUBSTITUTIONS

When you do not have exactly what the recipe calls for, here are some suggestions which are acceptable substitutes.

1 square cooking chocolate	=	3 tablespoons cocoa + 1 oz. butter
1 cup self raising flour	=	1 cup plain flour + 2 teaspoons of baking powder
1 cup sour milk	=	1 tablespoon lime juice or white vinegar + 1 cup milk
1 cup fresh milk	=	½ cup evaporated milk + ½ cup water
1 cup sour cream	=	1 cup warm milk + 1 tablespoon lime juice or white vinegar. Stirred to a thick consistency
Yeast compressed (1 oz.)	=	2 Teaspoons active dry yeast
1 fresh garlic clove	=	¼ teaspoon garlic powder
fresh green root ginger, grated	=	¼-½ teaspoon ground ginger

QUANTITIES PER HEAD

Appetizers	a variety of 4 - 6
Soup	5 servings to 1 quart
Sauces	10 servings to 1 pint
Fish	6 ozs. without bone
8 ozs. with bone	
Meat	4 ozs. without bone
6 ozs. with bone	
Green vegetables	6 servings 8 ozs
Potatoes	4 servings 8 ozs
Puddings/cold sweets	3 servings to 1 pint
Ices	10 servings to 1 quart
Poultry (chicken)	6 portions from a 4 lb. chicken
Poussin (chicken 3 - 4 weeks old)	1 portion

USEFUL KITCHEN EQUIPMENT

Cake tester	Blender
Poultry shears	Food chopper
Colander	Meat pounder
Rotary egg whisk	Nut grinder
Pastry blender	Pots, pans, casseroles
Pastry brush	Knives
Cheese graters	Sieves, rubber scrapers, bulb basters

Pots must be heavy bottomed. The best all purpose material is undoubtedly heavy enamelled cast iron. Copper pots are very satisfactory - the metal should be 1/8" thick and the handle should be made of iron. A kitchen should have round and oval casseroles. Saucepans various sizes - a skillet (sloping sides) and a sauté pan (straight sides).

Omelette Pan - This can be made of iron, with a long handle and a 2" sloping side and a 7" diameter bottom. This is perfect for 2 - 3 egg omelettes. When new, scrub with steel wool and scouring powder. Rinse and dry. Heat it and rub bottom with oil and let it stand overnight. Just before using, sprinkle 1 teaspoon of salt in the pan and rub with a paper towel.

Knives must be good quality, and kept in good condition: a 9" blade for chopping vegetables, a pointed knife for filleting, which should have a 6½" flexible blade. Knives for splitting chickens should have a 12" blade and should be heavy.
A carver should only be used for carving.

INDEX

P

Peppermint Sauce	48
Pickled Watermelon	62
Pickles & Preserves	
Bread & Butter Pickles	
Hot Peppers & Shallots	61
To Preserve Fresh Tomatoes	62
Pickney's Sweet	73
Pigeon Pie	22
Pigeons	
with Cabbage	21
with Pineapple	22
Pineapple	
Appetizer	2
Jam	64
Plantation Rum Punch	82
Pot Roast	31
Poor Man's Fillet	28
Pork Chops	
with Ginger Ale	28
with Pineapple	30
Pork Rind	3
Potato Salad	43
Preserves - see Pickles & Preserves	
Pudding	
Banana	68
Cornmeal	74
Otaheiti	73
Sweet Potato	74
Pumpkin	
Jam	64
Puff	38
Salad	43
Cream of Soup	9

Q

Quantities per Head	94

R

Rabbit Fricassee	30
Red Devil	62
Red Pea Soup	12
Red Stripe Batter for Fish	18
Rice & Peas	37
Rice or Macaroni Salad	43
Rio Cobre Mud	4
Ripe Banana Pie	68
Roast Chicken with Rice Stuffing	20
Roasted	
Breadfruit	1
Rabbit	30

Rum

Cake	80
Coffee Jelly	73
Sauce	48
Rump Steak Casserole	27

S

Sabayon Sauce	48
Salad	
Ackee	39
Avocado & Grapefruit	39
Breadfruit	40
Broad Bean	40
Callaloo	41
Carrot & Raisin	41
Chicken	41
Chocho	41
Conch	42
Creole	44
Cucumber & Sour Cream	42
Jamaican	42
Lobster	39
Macaroni	43
Onion	42
Potato	43
Pumpkin	43
Rice or Macaroni	43
Shrimp with coconut cream	44
String Bean	40
Sweet Pepper	43
Three Bean	40
Tropical	44
Tropical Fruit	70
Salmi of Duck	23
Salted Beef & Banana Casserole	26
Sauces - see Dressings & Sauces	
Sea Grape Jelly	65
Seasoned Breadfruit Chips	5
Shellfish - see Fish & Shellfish	
Shrimp	
Salad with Coconut Cream	44
with Pineapple	17
Sorrel Appetizer	82
Spare Ribs	29
Soursop Punch	83
Spicy Dressing	46
Stamp & Go	5
Starapple Appetizer	27
Stew Oxtail	25
Stewed Peas	31